100 PASSAGES

TO DEVELOP READING COMPREHENSION

This program is designed to enable average and better readers to develop into accomplished readers.

The material consists of 100 short, interesting reading selections of intrinsic value. The selections are arranged in ascending order of reading difficulty, beginning at the ninth grade reader level.

Each passage is accompanied by questions that elicit nine essential elements of the reading process. Thus, *100 Passages* enables teacher and student to concentrate on the student's *method* of reading, rather than on the *contents* of a particular passage. It develops conscious control over the thought processes which constitute efficient reading. Through nine distinct types of questions, the student learns to recognize the relationships of ideas, facts, and supporting material that make up the complex of communication.

Such better command of the thinking process leads naturally to significantly improved reading skill.

AUTHORS

ALLAN SACK

Formerly: Director, College Skills Center and Speed Reading Institute; Supervisor, Adult Reading Laboratory, College of the City of New York; Lecturer, Reading, Study Skills and Vocabulary Development, Extension Division and Graduate School of Business Administration, Rutgers University; American Institute of Banking; Currently: Consultant on Teacher Training.

JACK YOURMAN

Clinical Psychologist; Formerly: Director, College Skills Center and Speed Reading Institute. Consultant, New York Telephone Co., Port of New York Authority, United Nations. Lecturer, Rutgers University, American Institute of Banking; Associate Professor, Fordham University. Currently: Consultant, I.B.M., International Paper Company.

ACKNOWLEDGMENTS

We gratefully acknowledge the kind permission of the authors and publishers of the selections contained in this book.

Thomas Aquinas, *Commentary on Nichomachean Ethics*

Beauchamp, Mayfield, and West, *Science Problems 2 for Junior High School*, Scott, Foresman and Co.

Slater Brown, *World of the Wind*, The Bobbs-Merrill Co., Inc.

Rachel Carson, *The Sea Around Us*, Oxford University Press

Casner and Gabriel, *The Story of American Democracy*, Harcourt, Brace and Co.

Tobias Dantzig, *NUMBER The Language of Science*, Doubleday Anchor Books

Sebastian de Grazia, *Of Time, Work, and Leisure*, 20th Century Fund

Simon Dresner, *Heat*, Nelson Doubleday, Inc.

Bergan Evans, Redbook Magazine

Ralph M. Evans, *An Introduction to Color*, John Wiley and Sons, Inc.

H. J. Eysenck, *Uses and Abuses of Psychology*, Penguin Books, Inc.

Galbraith, *The Affluent Society*, Mentor Books, The New American Library of World Literature, Inc.

John E. Gibson, *Science Looks at Anger*

G. B. Harrison, *Shakespeare, Major Plays and the Sonnets*, Harcourt, Brace and Co.

S. I. Hayakawa, *Language, Meaning, and Maturity*, Harper and Row

Hermann Hesse, *Steppenwolf*, Frederick Ungar Publishing Co.

Lancelot Hogben, *Mathematics for the Millions*

Fred Hoyle, *Frontiers of Science*, Basic Books

William James, *Psychology*, Fawcett Publications, Inc.

Wendell Johnson, *People in Quandaries*

Joseph Wood Krutch, *The Modern Temper*, Harcourt, Brace, and World, Inc.

L. M. Myers, *American English*, Prentice-Hall

J. F. Reigart, *The Life of Robert Fulton*

Colin A. Ronan, *Radio and Radar Astronomy*, Nelson Doubleday, Inc.

Bertrand Russell, *A Free Man's Worship*, W. W. Norton and Co.

G. G. Scott, *General Biology*, Thomas Y. Crowell Co., Publishers

Charles L. Sherman, *The Science of Photography*, Nelson Doubleday, Inc.

Herbert Sorenson, *Psychology in Education*, McGraw-Hill Book Co., Inc.

Walter Sullivan, *We Are Not Alone*, McGraw-Hill Book Co., Inc.

Arthur Symons, *The Symbolist Movement in Literature*, E. P. Dutton and Co.

Douglas Tuomey, *The Home Mechanic*, The Macmillan Co.

William C. Vergara, *Science in Everyday Things*, Harper and Brothers

H. G. Wells, *Outline of History*, Doubleday

David Wechsler, *Measuring the I. Q.*, New York Times Magazine

William H. Whyte, Jr., *The Transients*, Ballantine Books

Editor: Barbara Pokrinchak, Ed.D.
Editorial Consultant: H. F. Criste

Printed in the United States of America.

ISBN: 0-89026-900-9

Order Number: 900

TO THE STUDENT

You have decided to put some of your time and energy into improving your reading comprehension. You have opened this book and are ready -- under the guidance of an instructor — to work with the passages within it.

You will get more benefit from your efforts if you have a clear idea of what is involved in improving comprehension, and how this book is intended to help you.

How do you improve comprehension? Improving comprehension is a process — a process of learning. This process has two main stages: understanding and application.

The essential thing to understand about comprehension is that your understanding of a passage is not *one* big thought in your mind, something like a wrapped-up package labeled "comprehension of a passage." Rather, your understanding of a passage is a number of *comprehensions.*

A passage is a collection of thoughts projected from one human being — the author — to you, the reader. True, these thoughts of the author may add up to one main idea which the author wishes to get across. But supporting this main idea are many smaller, subordinate ideas, details, and facts, each of which contributes to the overall thought of the passage. To understand, to "comprehend" a passage, you must understand each of the supporting ideas, and how they fit together.

To comprehend a passage fully, you must be able to understand other aspects of it. You may, for example, want to get clearly in mind what the real subject of the passage is, what the author's purpose was in writing the passage, even what effect the thought in the passage might have on some matter not even mentioned in the passage.

To grasp this idea that there are *comprehensions*, rather than one big comprehension in reading, you can think of a passage as a house. You can think of it in terms of its convenience. You can think about its impressiveness. You can think of each room in the house; or you can consider and understand separately its electrical system, its plumbing system, and so forth, Add all these separate comprehensions up, and you have your "comprehension" of the house as a whole, as an entity.

Coming back to reading, you can analyze, or think about, a passage in many ways. In *100 Passages*, we have chosen to work with the nine ways of thinking which we consider the most important.

These nine ways of thinking involve asking the following questions:

1. **What is the entire passage about?** We call the answer to this question the SUBJECT MATTER.

2. **What are the essential "points" of the passage?** Each main idea *which is supported by other material* we call a GENERALIZATION.

3. ***What are the specific facts or opinions used to clarify or to prove the main thought?*** We call the answer to this DETAIL.

4. ***What does the author want you to do or to believe?*** To get you to do something or to believe something, the author must first establish a Generalization. Once he has established his Generalization, he can then explicitly state, or strongly imply, a conclusion based upon it. Where a conclusion may be a call to some course of action, or a belief to be adopted, we call this kind of thinking FINDING THE SIGNIFICANCE.

5. ***What conclusions can be reasonably drawn from the Generalizations or the Details of the passage, which the author has not explicitly stated?*** We call this kind of thinking DRAWING CONCLUSIONS.

6. ***How can we apply the Conclusions we make about the passage to a new situation, not treated in the passage?*** We call this kind of thinking MAKING APPLICATIONS.

7. ***What is the feeling or attitude of the author toward the subject matter of the passage?*** We call the answer to this TONE AND ATTITUDE.

8. ***What is the precise meaning of a word as used in the passage?*** We call the answer to this VOCABULARY IN CONTEXT.

9. ***What can be observed about the organization of the passage? How are the generalizations related to each other? What kinds of proof does the author use?*** The answer to these questions involves understanding COMMUNICATION TECHNIQUES.

You will notice that questions 1 through 4 concern looking for the "plain sense" of a passage — what it says. Questions 5, 6, and 7 ask you to take further steps in thinking about the passage, to draw conclusions about it. Question 8, the vocabulary type of question, requires a very subtle type of comprehension, discriminating among shades of meaning of words used in the passage. Question 9 is concerned with considerations of form rather than content, with the HOW of the writing, not with the WHAT of it — with the way in which the written passage is constructed to communicate the author's message.

Once you have mastered these nine ways of thinking about a passage, you will have developed the analytical skills of reading. You can see the parts of a passage, and how these parts fit together. You can see the passage as a living tissue of ideas and facts which form a clear pattern in your mind. When you can do this with *100 Passages,* you will find yourself more expert at knowing what to look for and how to find what you want more quickly and accurately whenever you read.

This analytical approach can be applied to other kinds of "comprehension" besides reading. In the fine arts, for example, people wonder what there is to "understand" about paintings. When they are taught about the elements of painting — of line, color, tone, composition — they find that pictures become more meaningful.

So much for the *theory* of developing comprehension. As for the application — you are aware that all the understanding in the world won't make you skillful without practice. Here is how *100 Passages* is set up for you.

ORGANIZATION OF THIS BOOK

The 100 passages in this booklet have been culled from fields in which you would be expected to be able to read intelligently: the sciences - biology, chemistry, astronomy, physics, and geology; the humanities - philosophy, literature, criticism; and social studies - geography, history, law, and political economy. They are arranged in order of difficulty.

Accompanying each passage are questions about it. Questions are so arranged that you can work through them in either of two ways:

1. You will notice that each question is labeled as to which one of the nine types of thinking is required to solve it. Here are the types of questions, their symbols, and the decimal number that designates each:

Decimal	Type	Symbol
.1	SUBJECT MATTER	SM
.2	GENERALIZATION	G
.3	DETAIL	D
.4	SIGNIFICANCE	SIG
.5	CONCLUSION	C
.6	APPLICATION	A
.7	TONE AND ATTITUDE	T
.8	VOCABULARY	V
.9	COMMUNICATION TECHNIQUE	CT

    If your teacher wishes you to get practice in *one* of the nine types of thinking, you can answer each SUBJECT MATTER question or each GENERALIZATION question and move from passsage 1 to passage 2 to passage 3 and so on.

2. If your teacher wishes you to get experience with a variety of questions, you can stay with passage 1, do all the questions on it, and then move to passage 2, and so on.

Questions based on passages 91 through 100 are not labeled. In addition to answering each question, you are asked to designate the type of question, also. You can see that this kind of exercise is aimed at helping you to become as sophisticated as possible about reading.

Successful learning depends upon the proper attitude as well as on sound technique. If you are willing to do the thinking, make the effort, and *apply* the theory, your reading comprehension will improve.

My steamboat voyage to Albany and back has turned out rather more favorably than I had expected. The distance from New York to Albany is 150 miles. I ran it up within 32 hours and down in 30. I had a light breeze blowing against me the whole way both going and coming, and the voyage has been performed wholly by the power of the steam engine. I overtook many boats beating against the wind and parted with them as if they had been at anchor. The power of boats run by steam is now fully proved. The morning I left New York there were not, perhaps, thirty persons in the city who believed that the boat would ever move one mile per hour or be the least use.

———————————————— Questions for Passage #1 ————————————————

Find the best answer to each question. Circle the letter of your answer.

1.1
SUBJECT MATTER

Choose the best title for this passage.
A. The Success of the Steamboat
B. The Small Faith of Small People
C. The Effectiveness of the Steam Engine
D. A Trip to Albany
E. The Speed of the Steamboat

1.2
GENERALIZATION

The author's main thought is that
A. the steamboat voyage turned out more favorably than he had expected.
B. the author's steamboat trip was successful.
C. most people doubted that the steamboat would be of the least use.
D. the voyage was performed wholly by the power of the steam engine.
E. the steamboat, unlike a sailboat, can be used successfully with the wind against it.

1.5 (a)
CONCLUSION

Assuming that Poughkeepsie is midway between New York and Albany, and that Fulton's speed was constant, the leg of the author's trip from Poughkeepsie to New York must have taken
A. 5 hours.　　C. 10 hours.　　E. 20 hours.
B. 7 hours.　　D. 15 hours.

1.5 (b)
CONCLUSION

We can conclude from this passage that
A. many sailboats were at anchor when the author traveled the Hudson to Albany.
B. sailboats were having more difficulty with winds on the author's trip north than on the reverse leg of his journey.
C. no sailboat could have ever made Albany from New York in less than 32 hours.
D. sailboats were having difficulty with headwinds on both the author's upriver and downriver trips.
E. the distance from Albany to New York is shorter than that from New York to Albany.

1.9
COMMUNICATION TECHNIQUE

The author states that he had a "light breeze blowing against me the whole way both going and coming" to
A. provide local color in his description of the trip.
B. show why sails would not be an effective means of power.
C. indicate how pleasant his trip was.
D. prove the effectiveness of the steam engine.
E. do none of the above.

Men in all ways are better than they seem. They like flattery for the moment, but they know the truth for their own. It is foolish cowardice which keeps us from trusting them and speaking to them rude truth. They resent your honesty for an instant; they will thank you for it always. What is it we heartily wish of each other? Is it to be pleased and flattered? No, but to be convicted and exposed, to be shamed out of our nonsense of all kinds, and made men of, instead of ghosts and phantoms. We are weary of gliding ghostlike through the world, which is itself so slight and unreal. We crave a sense of reality, though it comes in strokes of pain.

———————————————— Questions for Passage #2 ————————————————

Find the best answer to each question. Circle the letter of your answer.

**2.1
SUBJECT MATTER**

This passage is mainly about
A. the value of men.
B. the need for trusting people.
C. the need for becoming a real person in a real world.
D. the need to be able to endure pain.
E. the need for truth in human relations.

**2.2
GENERALIZATION**

The author's main thought is that
A. flattery is always acceptable.
B. it is foolish cowardice which holds back our trust.
C. we must be shamed out of our nonsense.
D. reality with its pain can make men better.
E. honesty is sometimes resented but often admired.

**2.4
SIGNIFICANCE**

The author advises us to
A. stop being a ghost.
B. bear in mind that men like flattery.
C. face up to, and express, the truth.
D. stop being a coward even though it may make enemies.
E. thank people when they tell the unvarnished truth.

**2.9
COMMUNICATION
TECHNIQUE**

The author points out that "men are better than they seem" in order to show that
A. it is foolish for us to be cowardly and fear our neighbors.
B. we need not fear to tell people the truth.
C. people are not really looking for flattery.
D. they are weary of being ghosts.
E. we will find people grateful if we abandon nonsense of all kinds.

Blood vessels running all through the lungs carry blood to each air sac, or alveolus, and then back again to the heart. Only the thin wall of the air sac and the thin wall of a capillary are between the air and the blood. So oxygen easily diffuses from the air sacs through the walls into the blood, while carbon dioxide easily diffuses from the blood through the walls into the air sacs.

When blood is sent to the lungs by the heart, it has come back from the cells in the rest of the body. So the blood that goes into the wall of an air sac contains much dissolved carbon dioxide but very little oxygen. At the same time, the air that goes into the air sac contains much oxygen but very little carbon dioxide. You have learned that dissolved materials always diffuse from where there is more of them to where there is less. Oxygen from the air dissolves in the moisture on the lining of the air sac and diffuses through the lining into the blood. Meanwhile, carbon dioxide diffuses from the blood into the air sac. The blood then flows from the lungs back to the heart, which sends it out to all other parts of the body.

Soon after air goes into an air sac, it gives up some of its oxygen and takes in some carbon dioxide from the blood. To keep diffusion going as it should, this carbon dioxide must be gotten rid of. Breathing, which is caused by movements of the chest, forces the used air out of the air sacs in your lungs and brings in fresh air. The breathing muscles are controlled automatically so that you breathe at the proper rate to keep your air sacs supplied with fresh air. Ordinarily, you breathe about twenty-two times a minute. Of course, you breathe faster when you are exercising and slower when you are resting. Fresh air is brought into your lungs when you breathe in, or inhale, while used air is forced out of your lungs when you breathe out, or exhale.

Some people think that all the oxygen is taken out of the air in the lungs and that what we breathe out is pure carbon dioxide. But these ideas are not correct. Air is a mixture of gases that is mostly nitrogen. This gas is not used in the body. So the amount of nitrogen does not change as air is breathed in and out. But while air is in the lungs, it is changed in three ways: (1) About one-fifth of the oxygen in the air goes into the blood. (2) An almost equal amount of carbon dioxide comes out of the blood into the air. (3) Moisture from the linings of the air passages and air sacs evaporates until the air is almost saturated.

Find the best answer to each question. Circle the letter of your answer.

3.2 (a)
GENERALIZATION

In the respiratory process, the following action takes place:
A. diffusion of blood through capillary walls into air sacs.
B. diffusion of carbon dioxide through capillary and air sac walls into the blood.
C. diffusion of oxygen through the air sac and capillary walls into the blood.
D. exchange of alveoli and oxygen within air sacs.
E. none of the above.

3.2 (b)
GENERALIZATION

While air is in the lungs, it changes in the following way:
A. nitrogen is absorbed from the air.
B. about one-fifth of the carbon dioxide and about one-half of the oxygen in the air goes into the blood.
C. the moisture in the air is almost completely evaporated.
D. about one-fifth of the oxygen in the air goes into the blood and an equivalent amount of carbon dioxide enters the air from the blood.
E. none of the above changes are correct.

3.3
DETAIL

The number of times per minute that you breathe is
A. independent of your rate of exercise.
B. fixed at twenty-two times per minute.
C. influenced by your age and sex.
D. controlled automatically by an unspecified body mechanism.
E. dependent upon the amount of fresh air available to you at any given time.

3.5
CONCLUSION

The process by which carbon dioxide and oxygen are transferred does *not* depend on
A. the presence of nitrogen in the blood.
B. the muscles of the thoracic cavity.
C. the flow of blood.
D. the moisture in the air sac linings.
E. the process of diffusion.

3.7
TONE

The author's style in this passage can best be described as
A. informal and matter of fact.
B. pedantic.
C. impersonal.
D. matter of fact.
E. personal.

Another thing to remember in connection with concrete is that you are not allowed very much leeway for errors in either measurements or location. Once you have a solid mass of concrete set in place, it is going to stay there. You have a difficult job ahead of you if you try to remedy a mistake. Make very sure, before you fill the form, that everything is where and how you want it.

There are numerous rules regarding the proper mixing, handling, and finishing of concrete, but the essential one concerns the amount of water to use. The less water in the mix, the less the finished job will shrink. The less water used, the harder and more enduring the job after it has set.

The amateur concrete worker is plagued with two desires. One is to use enough water to have the concrete nice and soft and easy to push around. You have been warned against that. The second is to take off the wooden forms too early, to see what the job looks like. That is really fatal. If the forms are stripped off too soon, while the concrete is still "**green**," two things are likely to happen — you are almost sure to break off corners or edges, and you are likely to cause a major crack or defect in the body of the work. An excellent rule is to wait until you are sure the concrete is properly hardened, and then wait another day before removing the forms.

_____ Questions for Passage #4 _____

4.1
SUBJECT MATTER

The *best* title for this selection would be:
A. Rules for Working with Concrete.
B. Concrete and Its Uses.
C. Concrete, the Homeowner's Joy.
D. Concrete, a Test of Character.
E. How to Finish Concrete.

4.2
GENERALIZATION

Two of the main thoughts in this passage are (1) preparation of forms for the concrete must be thorough, and (2) forms must be allowed to remain on long enough. The third main idea is
A. taking off forms beforehand will probably cause a crack in the body of the work.
B. trying to make changes after concrete has been poured is not recommended.
C. mixing concrete properly will make it very hard and strong.
D. keeping concrete from shrinking as much as possible is desirable.
E. using as little water as possible is recommended.

4.4
SIGNIFICANCE

In mixing concrete, one of the desires the amateur must resist is to
A. break off a corner to see if the "green" has gone.
B. leave the form on too long.
C. strip off the forms a day after the concrete has properly hardened.
D. use too much water.
E. use too little water.

4.5
CONCLUSION

A human quality apparently *not* essential in someone who works with concrete is
A. carefulness.
B. patience.
C. self-control.
D. sense of spatial relations.
E. inventiveness.

4.8
VOCABULARY

By the concrete being too "green," the author means that the concrete has

A. become discolored because of its contact with the wooden forms.
B. become cracked.
C. not yet cured.
D. not dried out.
E. not settled in place.

4.9
COMMUNICATION TECHNIQUE

In instructing the reader in the intricacies of working with concrete, the author

A. gives specific instances of concrete work that went wrong.
B. allows the reader to find the solution to the problem from his own experience.
C. overstates the dire consequences of an error.
D. presents each problem and gives its solution.
E. understates the things that may go wrong.

5

By learning the life cycle of insects, scientists have found ways to control insect pests. The scientists who study insects are called entomologists. Entomologists discover what an insect is like in each stage of its development, where it lives, and what it eats. From these facts, a plan for controlling the insect can often be worked out. For example, the eggs of the stalk borer are laid on the stems of wild plants in late summer and stay there all winter. They hatch in May or June, and then the larvae bore into the stems of the wild plants. Later, the larvae move on to cultivated plants, where they again bore into the stems. In August the larvae become pupae in the stems of the cultivated plants. About three weeks later, they come out as adults and lay their eggs on wild plants. Burning the wild plants in late autumn or early spring greatly reduces the number of stalk borers that attack cultivated plants.

————————————— Questions for Passage #5 —————————————

5.1
SUBJECT MATTER

This paragraph centers on

A. the life cycles of insects.
B. scientists' use of their life cycles to control insect pests.
C. the life cycle of the stalk borer.
D. the role of wild plants in the control of the stalk borer.
E. the work of entomologists.

5.2
GENERALIZATION

Select the sentence which best summarizes the main idea of the passage.

A. The scientists who study insects are called entomologists.
B. Burning the wild plants in late autumn or early spring greatly reduces the number of stalk borers that attack cultivated plants.
C. By learning the life cycle of insects, scientists have found ways to control insect pests.
D. Entomologists discover what an insect is like in each state of its development, where it lives, and what it eats.
E. The extent of the damage caused by insects can only be established by entomologists.

Go on to next page.➤

5.3
DETAIL

Stalk borer adults appear
A. and lay their eggs in cultivated plants.
B. on wild plants reached by them as pupae.
C. on, and bore into, stems of wild plants.
D. on cultivated plants reached by them as larvae.
E. from pupae in the stems of wild plants.

5.9
COMMUNICATION
TECHNIQUE

The author describes the life cycle of the stalk borer to show
A. that entomologists are scientific.
B. how complicated are the stages of an insect's development.
C. the relationship between wild and cultivated plants.
D. why burning the wild plants in the late autumn or early spring will reduce the number of stalk borers.
E. how facts discovered about insects can be used to control them.

6

The soft pretzel, a lightly tanned delight, is quite distinct from its younger cousin, the hard and darker pretzel. Pretzel historians will tell you that this soft product originated in northern Italy about 600 A.D. A monk used the leftover strips of dough after baking bread by crossing the ends in familiar loops which represented children's arms folded in prayer. It was given to children who had learned their prayers as a little reward, or in Latin, "pretiola." The idea then caught on over the Alps in Austria where the word became corrupted to "brezel," "bretzel," and finally, pretzel.

————————————— Questions for Passage #6 —————————————

6.1
SUBJECT MATTER

This paragraph centers on
A. pretzels.
B. the difference between hard and soft pretzels.
C. pretzels and religion.
D. how we got the pretzel.
E. what the pretzel means.

6.2
GENERALIZATION

The main thought here is that
A. the creation of the pretzel showed the monk's ingenuity.
B. the giving of a reward to children for successful learning showed the monk's understanding of psychology.
C. the pretzel was created by a monk as a reward for children who had learned their prayers.
D. the "carrot" is preferable to the "stick" in encouraging learning.
E. expressed by none of the above.

6.3
DETAIL

The pretzel discussed by the author was
A. an inducement to learn prayers.
B. an historical accident.
C. first known as a "bretzel."
D. invented after the hard pretzel.
E. created by the monk mainly to prevent waste.

6.7
TONE

The author uses the term _pretzel historian_ to
A. cast doubt on the information in the paragraph.
B. designate the specific branch of historical research.
C. be sarcastic.
D. disclaim responsibility for the information in the passage.
E. introduce a humorous note.

The author mentions the *hard pretzel* to
A. prove that the light pretzel was invented before the dark pretzel.
B. define the pretzel under discussion.
C. show that the hard pretzel is coarser than the light pretzel.
D. interest the reader.
E. show his wide knowledge of pretzels.

7

Making a plaster patch a square foot or so in area is considerably more job than filling cracks, but there is no reason why the amateur should not attempt the repair if he makes his preparations properly.

Cut the edges around the opening cleanly, and wet them thoroughly. Make the mix of fresh plaster slightly stiffer (less water) than for the crack repair. Put on a base coat first, which means just enough to cover the **lath**, and see that it is below the face of the old edges. After this coat has set a little, mix another batch, slightly more fluid, and apply as a finish coat right over it, and smooth it out evenly with the old edges. This method is suggested because the weight of one full coating might be too much, and you would probably have some trouble keeping it in place on the lath.

To smooth off the finished coat nicely, take a straight, smooth piece of wood, with a more or less sharp edge long enough to span the patch, and work it across, back and forth over the new plaster. This will give you an even, smooth surface and avoid the necessity of troweling out any humps or filling in any depressions. In doing this kind of work, it is essential that the water be clean, and free from rust or dirt. If it is not, the patch will be discolored.

─────────────── Questions for Passage #7 ───────────────

7.1
SUBJECT MATTER

Select the most appropriate title for this selection.
A. Repairing Cracked Ceilings
B. Methods of Mixing Plaster
C. Finishing a Plaster Patch
D. How to Get a Smooth Surface on a Plaster Patch
E. How to Make a Plaster Patch

7.2
GENERALIZATION

In making a plaster patch, the passage does *not* say you should
A. make the mix of fresh plaster softer (more water) than in filling a crack.
B. use a straight piece of wood to work across the patch.
C. use clean water.
D. put on a base coat of plaster first.
E. put a second coat over the first coat.

7.3
DETAIL

One of the important details mentioned in the passage makes it apparent that
A. the first coating of plaster should be brought up even with the face of the edges of the patch.
B. the ability of lath to retain plaster is limited.
C. it is advisable to trowel out lumps and fill in depressions to obtain a smooth-surfaced patch.
D. the amateur need have no fear about his ability to make a plaster patch.
E. plaster is prone to develop breaks and cracks.

Go on to next page. ➤

This passage has probably been taken from
A. a technical manual for plasterers.
B. an article in an encyclopedia about plaster.
C. a newspaper advertisement.
D. a "how-to-do-it" article in a magazine for homeowners.
E. instructions on a bag of plaster.

By "lath" the author means
A. a machine for shaping an article of wood.
B. wooden lattice work used as the foundation for plaster.
C. the foam or froth resulting from the mixing of plaster and water.
D. the irregular cracks in the old plaster.
E. the paint coating over the old plaster.

8

(1) Let us look briefly at the main organs — the lungs. (2) They let oxygen from the air into the blood and give out carbon dioxide. (3) Except for the parts taken up by the heart and the windpipe, the lungs fill almost the entire chest cavity. (4) Inside each lung the bronchial tubes fork like the branches of a tree. (5) That is, they divide and subdivide to form smaller and smaller tubes until they reach every part of the lungs. (6) The linings of all these air passages are covered with tiny living hairs, called cilia, that move back and forth. (7) The movements of the cilia sweep dust and other unwanted materials up and out of the air passages. (8) At the ends of the very smallest bronchial tubes, the air goes into many tiny cup-shaped parts. (9) These are the air sacs, or alveoli, which are arranged around the tubes somewhat like a bunch of grapes on a stem. (10) Scientists have estimated that a person's lungs contain about 600 million air sacs. (11) If the linings of all these sacs formed a single sheet, it would cover the walls of a room 20 feet long, 15 feet wide, and 10 feet high. (12) The lungs are very light, spongy organs because they contain so many bronchial tubes and air sacs.

——————————— Questions for Passage #8 ———————————

This passage is mainly about
A. startling facts about the lungs.
B. the structure of the respiratory system.
C. the functioning of man's breathing apparatus.
D. the structure of the lungs.
E. the organs of the chest cavity.

The body rids itself of foreign particles which get into the lungs principally by means of
A. hairs.
B. alveoli.
C. bronchial linings.
D. coughing.
E. an undisclosed mechanism.

The substance that appears to take up most of the space of the chest cavity is that comprising the
A. windpipe.
B. air sacs.
C. heart.
D. cilia.
E. bronchi.

8.9
COMMUNICATION
TECHNIQUE

Which one of the following sentences from the passage deals with the functioning of the lungs?

A. sentence (2)　　　　D. sentence (8)

B. sentence (3)　　　　E. sentence (12)

C. sentence (4)

9

Communication between villages and the nearest town was poor. Roads were bad; there was some attempt to keep them in order, but as each parish was responsible for its own section of road, the state of repair depended on the zeal of the parish officers. There was, however, little wheeled traffic except for farm coaches used by men of wealth. Most traffic was by means of pack horses. Travelers rode on horseback or walked. Since communication was so difficult, the local markets, held weekly at the nearest town, or the fairs, held annually at the greater cities, became important places for the exchange of goods of all kinds.

—————————————— Questions for Passage #9 ——————————————

9.1
SUBJECT MATTER

This passage is primarily about

A. traveling.　　　　D. roads.

B. fairs.　　　　E. the exchange of goods.

C. communication.

9.2
GENERALIZATION

In this passage the author's conclusion that local markets and fairs were important is based on his statement that

A. communication between villages and towns was poor.

B. roads were bad.

C. there was little wheeled traffic.

D. exchanges of goods took place at the markets.

E. markets and fairs were held periodically.

9.3
DETAIL

Most traffic was not on wheels because

A. most people could not afford this means of travel.

B. springless coaches were uncomfortable.

C. pack horses were better than coaches.

D. roads were so bad.

E. of an unspecified reason.

9.5
CONCLUSION

Poor roads were probably so because of

A. the costliness of reforms.

B. politics on a parish level.

C. the competition between parishes.

D. the paucity of traffic.

E. the indolence of local authorities.

9.9
COMMUNICATION
TECHNIQUE

The author's statement about the importance of markets and fairs is

A. a conclusion he draws on the basis of his main thought.

B. an interesting fact he includes, although it does not bear strictly on the subject matter of the passage.

C. apparently contradicted by the main thought.

D. a historical development which took place after the time in which the main events of the passage occurred.

E. a proof he uses to establish his main thought.

Man, even in the lower stages of development, possesses a faculty which, for want of a better name, I shall call *Number Sense.* This faculty permits him to recognize that something has changed in a small collection when, without his direct knowledge, an object has been removed from or added to the collection.

Number sense should not be confused with counting, which is probably of a much later vintage, and involves, as we shall see, a rather intricate mental process. Counting, so far as we know, is an attribute exclusively human, whereas some brute species seem to possess a rudimentary number sense akin to our own. At least, such is the opinion of competent observers of animal behavior, and the theory is supported by a weighty mass of evidence.

Many birds, for instance possess such a number sense. If a nest contains four eggs, one can safely be taken; but when two are removed, the bird generally deserts. In some unaccountable way the bird can distinguish two from three. But this faculty is by no means confined to birds. In fact, the most striking instance we know is that of the insect called the "solitary wasp." The mother wasp lays her eggs in individual cells and provides each egg with a number of live caterpillars on which the young feed when hatched. Now, the number of victims is remarkably constant for a given species of wasp. Some species provide 5, others, 12, others again as high as 24 caterpillars per cell. But most remarkable is the case of the *Genus Eumenus,* a variety in which the male is much smaller than the female. In some mysterious way the mother knows whether the egg will produce a male or a female grub and apportions the quantity of food accordingly; she does not change the species or size of the prey, but if the egg is male, she supplies it with five victims; if female, with ten.

The regularity in the action of the wasp and the fact that this action is connected with a fundamental function in the life of the insect make this last case less convincing than the one which follows. Here the action of the bird seems to border on the conscious:

A squire was determined to shoot a crow which made its nest in the watchtower of his estate. Repeatedly he tried to surprise the bird, but in vain: at the approach of man the crow would leave its nest. From a distant tree it would watchfully wait until the man had left the tower and then return to its nest. One day the squire hit upon a ruse: two men entered the tower, one remained within, the other came out and went on. But the bird was not deceived: it kept away until the man within came out. The experiment was repeated on the succeeding days with two, three, then four men, yet without success. Finally, five men were sent: as before, all entered the tower, and one remained while the other four came out and went away. Here the crow lost count. Unable to distinguish between four and five, it promptly returned to its nest.

10.2
GENERALIZATION

The main idea of this passage is that

A. man's rudimentary number sense is found in lower species.

B. counting is not to be confused with number sense.

C. birds have a limited number sense.

D. animals cannot count.

E. number sense is a primitive form of counting.

10.3 (a)
DETAIL

Counting is different from number sense in that counting is

A. dependent on simpler mental activity.

B. farther up the evolutionary scale.

C. found in animals as well as man.

D. present in animals on the basis of much evidence.

E. the ability to distinguish differences in small sets of objects.

10.3 (b)
DETAIL

The author feels that the number sense displayed by *Genus Eumenus* is

A. more remarkable than that of a crow.

B. on a par with that of a crow.

C. less convincing an instance than that displayed by the crow because it seems to be instinctive.

D. actually not an instance of what the author is discussing because it is tied to a regular pattern of responses.

E. restricted to the female of this species.

10.3 (c)
DETAIL

The crow was finally deceived because

A. it was not afraid of the men in the tower.

B. it did not have a number sense.

C. four men left the tower.

D. it could not distinguish between four and five.

E. it was evening and the crow was unable to count the hunters.

10.5
CONCLUSION

We can conclude from this passage that number sense in animals appears to be

A. restricted to about one dozen species or less.

B. related directly to preservation of self or offspring.

C. present chiefly in winged creatures.

D. akin to a faculty possessed by men in all stages of development.

E. as intricate as counting.

The meridians of longitude are imaginary great circles drawn from pole to pole around the earth. By international agreement, the meridian of longitude passing through Greenwich, England, is numbered zero. The earth is divided into 360 degrees, and the meridians are numbered east and west from Greenwich. There are 180 degrees of longitude east of Greenwich and 180 degrees in the westerly direction. New York has a longitude of 74 degrees west (74° W.) which means that it lies on the 74th meridian west of Greenwich.

Since the sun appears to travel around the earth in 24 hours, it will move 360/24 or 15 degrees in one hour. This reasoning can be used by navigators to determine their longitude. Imagine that we have set sail from Greenwich, England, after having set a very accurate clock, or chronometer, to the local Greenwich time. As we travel westward toward New York, we notice that the sun is going "slower" than our chronometer. At the time that our timepiece reads 12 o'clock, the sun has not quite reached the zenith. As a matter of fact, when our clock reads noon, what it really means is that it's noon in Greenwich, England. Our clock continues to tell us the time, not at our present location, but at Greenwich. Let us wait until the sun is directly overhead (noon at our location) and then read the time on our clock. Suppose it reads 1 o'clock. This means that there is one hour's difference in time between our longitude and that of Greenwich. As we mentioned earlier, this corresponds to exactly 15 degrees of longitude, so our longitude must be 15° W. The world is divided into 24 time zones, and each zone corresponds to 15 degrees of longitude. New York is approximately 5 time zones west of Greenwich, so the time difference must be about 5 hours. By maintaining chronometers on Greenwich time, ships can determine their longitude on any sunny day by merely noting the difference in hours between Greenwich time and local sun time and multiplying this difference by 15 degrees.

Of course, longitude gives only half of the information needed to determine our precise location. We must also know our latitude, which tells us how far we are north or south of the Equator. The Equator is the zero line for the measurement of latitude. Circles are drawn parallel to the Equator to indicate other values of latitude. There are 90 degrees of south latitude. In the Northern Hemisphere, there is a star called Polaris almost directly over the North Pole. This makes it possible to determine the latitude of a given point by setting our sextant to measure the angle between Polaris, the North Star, and the horizon. Mathematicians tell us that this angle is equal to the latitude at the point in question.

To get an idea of our location, therefore, we need to know local time, Greenwich time, and the angle between Polaris and the horizon.

11.2 (a)
GENERALIZATION

In order to establish the "fix" or precise location of a ship, the navigator must know
A. his latitude.
B. both his latitude and longitude.
C. local time.
D. the number of degrees he is east or west of Greenwich.
E. his longitude.

11.2 (b)
GENERALIZATION

In order to determine latitude, the navigator must know
A. Greenwich time and local time.
B. a good deal of mathematics.
C. the angle between Polaris and the horizon.
D. Greenwich time, local time, and the angle between Polaris and the horizon.
E. his precise location.

11.3 (a)
DETAIL

A navigator's chronometer will always show
A. local time.
B. noon time.
C. Greenwich time.
D. sun time.
E. the position east or west of Greenwich.

11.3 (b)
DETAIL

In relation to the earth, the sun will move
A. 7,000 miles per hour.
B. twice as far as Polaris.
C. 1/48th of the world's circumference.
D. fifteen degrees in one hour.
E. thirty degrees in one hour.

11.5
CONCLUSION

It can be inferred from the third paragraph that the number of degrees of latitude in the Northern Hemisphere is

A. 18°.   D. 72°.
B. 36°.   E. 90°.
C. 54°.

11.6
APPLICATION

Assume the circumference of the earth to be 21,600 nautical miles. Ten degrees of longitude at the equator would then equal
A. 500 miles.
B. 600 miles.
C. 1,000 miles.
D. 1,200 miles.
E. an amount which cannot be determined from the data in the passage.

Divide the human race into twenty parts, and there will be nineteen composed of those who work with their hands, and who will never know that there was a Locke in the world; in the twentieth part remaining, how few are there who can read, and among those who can, there will be twenty who read romances, to one who studies science. The number of those who can think is excesssively small.

───────────── Questions for Passage #12 ─────────────

12.2
GENERALIZATION

The main idea of this passage is that
A. too few people read Locke.
B. too many people study romances.
C. too few people know about Locke.
D. too few people can read.
E. too few people can think.

12.3
DETAIL

According to the author, out of every 1,000 persons, the largest approximate number who can think can be put at
A. 1 to 2 persons.   D. 20 to 50 persons.
B. 3 to 6 persons.   E. 50 to 100 persons.
C. 20 to 40 persons.

12.7
TONE

The author's attitude toward those who know about Locke is one of
A. respect.   D. wonder.
B. disdain.   E. affection.
C. adulation.

13

At this time the state of South Carolina was having hard times. Year after year the soil had been planted to the same crop. It was farmed by uneducated and careless slaves, and the planters knew little about soil conservation. Because the soil was beginning to wear out, crops were smaller. The younger people were not satisfied to raise cotton on the poor soil of the old South. Many of them moved westward and started cotton plantations in Alabama and Mississippi. Moreover, so much cotton had been shipped to factories in England and New England that they had as much cotton as they could use. This brought the price of cotton down. More and more slaves were needed to work on the new and larger plantations, and higher and higher prices were demanded for them. Planters found their expenses rising and their incomes from the sale of cotton reduced. Hard times had come to South Carolina.

───────────── Questions for Passage #13 ─────────────

13.1
SUBJECT MATTER

The subject of this passage is
A. ignorance of planters about farming.
B. economic rivalry in the South.
C. the Secession — its causes.
D. deterioration of the soil in South Carolina.
E. economic difficulties of South Carolina.

**13.2
GENERALIZATION**

Which of the following sentences comes closest to summarizing the main idea of the passage?
A. Hard times had come to South Carolina.
B. Planters found their expenses rising and their incomes from the sale of cotton reduced.
C. The soil was farmed by uneducated and careless slaves.
D. Year after year the soil of South Carolina had been planted with the same crop.
E. Because the soil was beginning to wear out, crops were smaller.

**13.3
DETAIL**

In discussing the economy of South Carolina, one of the author's assumptions is that the reader understands
A. the feelings of young people.
B. the lack of knowledge on the part of planters and slaves.
C. farming methods in use at the time.
D. the law of supply and demand.
E. why more slaves were needed.

**13.5
CONCLUSION**

Plantations grew in size in South Carolina principally because
A. demand for cotton had slackened.
B. crops became diversified.
C. planters grew richer.
D. soil was less productive.
E. places had to be found for young people.

**13.9
COMMUNICATION
TECHNIQUE**

The fact that cotton prices were falling is mentioned by the author to show that
A. cotton shipments should have been regulated.
B. poorer soil produced poorer quality crops.
C. the planters were having hard times.
D. the planter's ignorance of soil management resulted in economic loss.
E. there were reasons why young peple moved westward.

14

As to living a spiritual life, he never tackled that problem. Some men who accept spiritual beliefs, try to live up to them daily; other men, who reject such beliefs, try sometimes to smash them. My father would have disagreed with both kinds entirely. He took a more distant attitude. It disgusted him when atheists attacked religion; he thought they were vulgar. But he also objected to have religion make demands upon him — he felt that religion too was vulgar, when it tried to stir up men's feelings. It had its own proper field of activity, and it was all right there, of course; but there was one place religion should let alone, and that was a man's soul. He especially loathed any talk of walking hand in hand with his Savior. And if he had ever found the Holy Ghost trying to soften his heart, he would have regarded its behavior as distinctly uncalled for; even ungentlemanly.

Go on to next page. ➤

14.5
CONCLUSION

The author's father probably felt that organized religion was
A. acceptable if kept within certain bounds.
B. concerned with man's salvation.
C. a threat which should be eliminated.
D. a spiritual problem which did not concern him.
E. unnecessary.

14.7
TONE

The author's treatment of his father's religious attitudes basically reflects
A. amusement.   D. disappointment.
B. disapproval.   E. sarcasm.
C. irreverence.

15

The other terror that scares us from self-trust is our consistency; a reverence for our past act or word because the eyes of others have no other data for computing our orbit than our past acts, and we are loath to disappoint them. But why should you keep your head over your shoulder? Why drag about this monstrous corpse of your memory lest you contradict somewhat you have stated in this or that public place? Suppose you should contradict yourself; what then? It seems to be a rule of wisdom never to rely on your memory alone, scarcely even in acts of pure memory, but to bring the past for judgment into the thousand-eyed present, and live ever in a new day. Trust your emotion.

_____ Questions for Passage #15 _____

15.2
GENERALIZATION

The main idea of this passage is that
A. being inconsistent will help us to build self-confidence.
B. our emotion is a better guide to decisions than our memory
C. our memory is deceptive.
D. we should not be afraid to offend or shock others by contradicting ourselves.
E. our concern with being consistent prevents us from trusting our judgment in the present.

15.4
SIGNIFICANCE

Instead of "keeping our head over our shoulder," we should
A. trust our emotion rather than our judgment.
B. not allow our recollection of our past acts to determine our present acts or words.
C. be consistently inconsistent.
D. shrug off public statements.
E. ignore the past.

15.5
CONCLUSION

The author has introduced an apparent contradiction into the passage by his statement about
A. terror and consistency.
B. corpse and memory.
C. judgment and emotion.
D. never relying on pure memory.
E. speaking in public and contradicting ourselves.

15.7
TONE

The author's style in this passage seems best characterized as
A. respectful.   D. persuasive.
B. didactic.   E. none of the above.
C. diffident.

15.8
VOCABULARY

The author calls memory a "monstrous corpse" because
A. it hinders our fresh appraisal of the current situation.
B. he feels that it is useless to remember what is past.
C. we are terrified by the fear of forgetting.
D. it gives others a way of judging us.
E. it stifles our emotion.

16

Clothes poles and clothes dryers are quite often **out of plumb**, and nothing makes a yard look untidier than these appurtenances if they are out of a vertical position. They can be taken up and a hole dug of the proper depth, which is about 3 inches greater than the diameter of the pole. The pole should be reset, plumbed up and fastened temporarily by light strips of wood nailed to it and to stakes driven into the ground. Concrete should be poured all around and tamped into place and allowed to set thoroughly before the temporary bracing is removed.

—————————————— Questions for Passage #16 ——————————————

16.1
SUBJECT MATTER

A good title for this selection would be
A. Ugly Backyards.
B. The Use of Concrete in Setting Clothes Poles.
C. How to Align Clothes Poles.
D. How to Set a Clothes Pole Straight.
E. Clothes Poles and Clothes Dryers.

16.2
GENERALIZATION

The best general statement giving the sense of this passage is that
A. the best way to straighten clothes poles is to take them out and reinstall them.
B. the key to working with clothes poles is to brace them temporarily.
C. backyard appurtenances should be installed by using concrete.
D. clothes poles can be set straight by following several steps.
E. clothes poles are too often not installed correctly.

16.3
DETAIL

In digging a hole in which to set the pole of a clothes dryer, the hole should be
A. as deep as the diameter plus three inches.
B. three inches deep.
C. as wide as the diameter of the pole plus three inches.
D. the thickness of the pole through the diameter plus three inches.
E. none of the above.

16.8
VOCABULARY

By "out of plumb" the author means
A. not vertical.   D. bent.
B. not horizontal.   E. too short.
C. out of line.

16.9
COMMUNICATION
TECHNIQUE

The function of sentence 1 in this passage is to
A. introduce the subject of home beautification.
B. give specific instructions about the installation of clothes dryers.
C. serve as transition between this passage and matters previously discussed.
D. give the real reason why the author took the trouble to write the passage.
E. show why the rest of the passage should be read.

Uppermost in a tourist's imagination is the fact that Yucatan is still the tranquil mystical land of the Mayas, so full of timeless legend and superstition that fact and fantasy can not be told apart. For all the Spanish Conquest it is now, as it has always been, the home of the Mayas, those slim little sad-eyed Indians with drooping eyelids — a dark skinned and fragile-looking race. As with all ancient peoples, the past is as real and evident to the mind as the present. The Mayas worship the God of their conquerors. But in the ruined cities of the jungle, they still secretly burn candles to the old idols.

————————— Questions for Passage #17 —————————

17.1
SUBJECT MATTER

The title below that best expresses the idea of this passage is:
A. Yucatan, Home of the Mayas.
B. The Ancient Religion of the Mayas.
C. The Persistence of Mayan Culture.
D. Effects of the Spanish Conquest.
E. Legends of Yucatan.

17.3
DETAIL

The people of Yucatan publicly worship
A. Mayan gods.
B. ancient idols.
C. Spanish conquistadors.
D. the Christian Deity.
E. only when forced to.

17.9
COMMUNICATION
TECHNIQUE

The author of this passage achieves his purpose by depending mainly upon
A. carefully chosen adjectives and adverbs.
B. carefully reasoned proofs which support his main thought.
C. a series of well-supported statements which carry conviction because they are stated categorically.
D. the reader's lack of familiarity with the subject matter.
E. none of the above.

The coastal area of North Africa is almost as pleasant as southern California, with hot, dry summers, and consistently heavy rains in winter. The forested mountains of Morocco and Algeria have a heavy winter snowfall, and excellent skiing grounds. Temperatures in the coastland's higher altitudes fall below freezing on winter nights. South of the mountains and plateaus the true desert begins. It is **not a continuous sea of land**; some parts are great stretches of picturesque dunes, but others are rim rock and gravel, not at all flat, and one may travel for days and see scarcely any sand. Rains fall rarely, though then in such large doses that bivouac commanders should take care not to make camp in a ravine. Winter nights are bitterly cold.

────────────── Questions for Passage #18 ──────────────

18.1
SUBJECT MATTER

A good title for this selection would be:
A. Responsibilities of Bivouac Commanders.
B. Geography of North Africa.
C. The Coastal Region of North Africa.
D. Floods and Droughts.
E. Climate of North Africa.

18.2
GENERALIZATION

The main thought of this passage is that
A. the climatic conditions of North Africa have great similarity to our own country.
B. North Africa includes a coastal area like southern California, forested mountains, and true desert.
C. the coastal area of North Africa is almost as pleasant as southern California.
D. bivouac commanders should be prepared for the advantages and disadvantages of the North African topography.
E. the true desert is varied in its topography.

18.3
DETAIL

South of the mountains and plateaus
A. rains fall consistently in winter.
B. rains fall rarely.
C. rains, when they fall, fall in negligible quantities.
D. no rains ever fall.
E. none of the above are true.

18.4
SIGNIFICANCE

The author suggests that the traveler not sleep in ravines because
A. the cold of winter nights settles to the lowest part of the plains.
B. the ravines are rocky and therefore unsuitable for camping.
C. sudden rain floods could drown the traveler.
D. morning dew settles into the ravines, making them wet and uncomfortable.
E. of none of the above.

18.8
VOCABULARY

The author portrays the desert south of the mountains as "not a continuous sea of land." By that phrase the author means that
A. the desert is never wet.
B. the desert is unlike the sea because its scenery is varied.
C. the hills of the desert do not resemble the waves of the sea.
D. the desert extends from horizon to horizon just like the sea.
E. the desert is unlike the sea because of its dryness and barrenness.

The child is not just young — it is not simply a matter of his having lived a shorter time than the adult. The fact that we should always keep in mind in considering children is that they are incomplete beings, that they are growing and developing, that they are men in the making, and the making is a very active process. Roughly speaking, this activity is in inverse ratio to the age of the child. For example, there is a greater difference between a child of five and one of two than there is between a child of five and one of eight. Again, there is a greater difference between a child of ten and one of fifteen than between a man of thirty and one of forty. These differences express themselves not so much in variations of size or form but most distinctly in function, that is, in the varying ability of the individual to adapt himself to his environment. In short, the most marked difference between the child of two and that of five, and the child of five and one of eight, lies in the capacity for social adaptation of each one, and this is equally true all the way along the ladder of years.

_____ Questions for Passage #19 _____

**19.5
CONCLUSION**

In comparing the thirties in a person's life with his twenties, we can conclude that

A. more "growth" takes place.

B. less "growth" takes place.

C. an equal amount of "growth" takes place.

D. growth of a different kind takes place.

E. none of the above are true.

**19.6
APPLICATION**

Of the following five evidences of growth in a child, which do you feel would be of *least* concern to the author?

A. achieving sufficient coordination to catch a ball.

B. being accepted into a club.

C. attaining his father's height.

D. learning to bring in the newspaper.

E. learning to skate.

**19.9
COMMUNICATION
TECHNIQUE**

In discussing aging and growth, the author develops his passage by

A. discussing various aspects of growth in the life of child, adolescent, and adult.

B. devoting so much space to the factor rate of growth that he fails to make his point.

C. making unsupported generalizations about three specific aspects of growth.

D. making a general statement and then marshalling proofs to support it.

E. advancing a definition of growth and then elaborating it by making further distinctions within the definition.

The day had gone by just as days go by. I had killed it in accordance with my **primitive and retiring way of life.** I had worked for an hour or two and perused the pages of old books. I had had pains for two hours, as elderly people do. I had taken a powder and been very glad when the pains consented to disappear. I had lain in a hot bath and absorbed its kindly warmth. Three times the post had come with undesired letters and circulars to look through. I had done my breathing exercises, but found it convenient today to omit the thought exercises. I had been for an hour's walk and seen the loveliest feathery cloud patterns pencilled against the sky. That was very delightful. So was the reading of the old books. So was the lying in the warm bath. But, taken all in all, it had not been exactly a day of rapture. No, it had not even been a day brightened with happiness and joy. Rather, it had been just one of those days which for a long while now had fallen to my lot; the moderately pleasant, the wholly bearable and tolerable, lukewarm days of a discontented middle-aged man; days without special pains, without special cares, without particular worry, without despair, days which put the question quietly of their own accord whether the time has not come to follow the example of Adalbert Stifter and have a fatal accident while shaving.

———————————————— Questions for Passage #20 ————————————————

20.2
GENERALIZATION

The storyteller considers having a fatal accident because
A. his surroundings are dreary.
B. he has suicidal tendencies.
C. his life has lost meaning.
D. he has a fatal disease.
E. he is old.

20.8
VOCABULARY

By his "primitive, retiring way of life," the author refers to a life
A. retricted to biological functions.
B. devoid of cultural interests.
C. of simple experiences not dependent upon civilization.
D. in which social contact, with its attendant complex relationships, is missing.
E. of deep emotion.

20.9
COMMUNICATION
TECHNIQUE

The author starts seven sentences with the phrase "I had . . ." He does this
A. because ne is a poor writer.
B. to emphasize that the story is told in the first person.
C. to show that, not being a writer, he is unskilled with words.
D. to emphasize his loneliness.
E. to reflect the monotony of his own life.

21

Literary persons, even the greatest, are seldom spectacular. Those who lead lives of heroic action have neither the time nor usually the desire, even if they have the ability, to express themselves in writing. Those who gallop down valleys of death do not sing about that experience; they leave it to gentle poets living comfortably in country retreats. Moreover, to be a great writer one must spend more of one's time at a table in the laborious and wholly **prosaic** act of writing. Few writers attract a Boswell, and unless the details of their lives, their sayings, and their oddities happen to be preserved in writing, they soon become little more than a name. Even with all the elaborate apparatus of modern publicity, few readers could without notice write more of the biography of any living writer than could be contained on a postcard. The word is always so much greater than the man.

————————————————— Questions for Passage #21 —————————————————

21.2
GENERALIZATION

The main idea of this passage is that
A. most literary men would prefer to lead lives of action.
B. what writers write is more significant than what they do.
C. the man of action is often a poor writer.
D. most readers are uninformed about the lives of writers.
E. most writers are merely names to the public.

21.3
DETAIL

Most men who lead a life of heroic action do not write because
A. they are often illiterate.
B. they are too modest.
C. they are either too busy, uninterested, or both.
D. writing requires a gentleness which men of action lack.
E. of none of the above reasons.

21.5
CONCLUSION

The author's remarks about "modern publicity" imply that
A. publishing houses have wasted their time trying to publicize writers.
B. publicity today is more effective in making lives of writers well known.
C. most readers are immune to the apparatus of modern publicity.
D. publicity does little good.
E. none of the above are true.

21.8 (a)
VOCABULARY

"Those who gallop down the valleys of death" refers to people who
A. have known suffering.
B. do not fear death.
C. lead daring lives of action.
D. are modest about their experiences.
E. are literary in their pursuits.

21.8 (b)
VOCABULARY

The word "prosaic" as used by the author means most nearly
A. unpoetical.
B. exhausting.
C. creative.
D. dull.
E. romantic.

Geologists have been studying volcanoes for a long time. Though they have learned a great deal, they still have not discovered the causes of volcanic action. They know that the inside of the earth is very hot, but they are not sure exactly what causes the great heat. Some geologists have thought that the heat is caused by the great pressure of the earth's outer layers. Or the heat may be left from the time when the earth was formed. During the last sixty years scientists have learned about radium, uranium, thorium, and other radioactive elements. These give out heat all the time as they change into other elements. Many scientists now believe that much of the heat inside the earth is produced by radioactive elements.

Whatever the cause of the heat may be, we do know that the earth gets hotter the farther down we dig. In deep mines and oil wells the temperature rises about 1° F. for each 50 feet. At this rate the temperature 40 miles below the earth's surface would be over 4,000° F. This is much hotter than necessary to melt rock. However, the pressure of the rock above keeps most materials from melting at their usual melting points. Geologists believe that the rock deep in the earth may be plastic, or putty-like. In other words, the rock yields slowly to pressure but is not liquid. But if some change in the earth's crust releases the pressure, the rock melts. Then the hot, liquid rock can move up toward the surface.

When the melted rock works its way close to the earth's crust, a volcano may be formed. The melted rock often contains steam and other gases under great pressure. If the rock above gives way, the pressure is released. Then the sudden expansion of the gases causes explosions. These blow the melted rock into pieces of different sizes and shoot them high in the air. Here they cool and harden into volcanic ash and cinders. Some of this material falls around the hole made in the earth's surface. The melted rock may keep on rising and pour out as lava. In this way, volcanic ash, cinders, and lava build up the cone-shaped mountains that we call volcanoes.

—————— Questions for Passage #22 ——————

22.1
SUBJECT MATTER

The subject of this passage is the
A. formation of volcanoes.
B. results of volcanic action.
C. work of geologists.
D. interior of the earth.
E. causes of the earth's internal heat.

22.3
DETAIL

The cause for the heat in the interior of the earth is
A. radioactive elements.
B. the great pressure of the earth.
C. not determined.
D. the heat remaining from the formation of the earth.
E. volcanic action in the interior of the earth.

22.5
CONCLUSION

From the information given in the passage, most minerals would melt fastest
A. at 4000° F. at sea level.
B. at 4000° F., 5000 feet below sea level.
C. in the absence of oxygen.
D. at the exact center of the earth at 4000°.
E. at 4000° F., 5000 feet above sea level.

Go on to next page. ➤

22.6
APPLICATION

If the temperature at the earth's surface is twenty degrees Fahrenheit, the temperature in a coal mine 500 feet below the surface would, in degrees, be

A. 30.
B. 40.
C. 50.

D. 120.
E. 500.

23

I am not so naive, however, as to believe that sex is responsible for this unfortunate plight of the American woman. I am not a **feminist,** but I am an individualist. I do not believe there is any important difference between men and women — certainly not as much as there may be between one woman and another or one man and another. There are plenty of women — and men, for that matter — who would be completely fulfilled in being allowed to be as lazy as possible. If someone will ensconce them in a pleasant home and pay their bills, they ask no more of life. It is quite all right for these men and women to live thus so long as fools can be found who will pay so much for nothing much in return. Gigolos, male and female, are to be found in every class and in the best of homes. But when a man does not want to be a gigolo, he has the freedom to go out and work and create as well as he can. But a woman has not. Even if her individual husband lets her, tradition in society is against her.

_____ Questions for Passage #23 _____

23.2
GENERALIZATION

The author feels that women
A. are against tradition.
B. prefer to be cared for.
C. feel that their husbands are their allies.
D. can justifiably blame men for their lack of freedom.
E. are not free to be self-supporting.

23.3
DETAIL

The chief obstacle to freedom of women is
A. social mores.
B. opposition of their husbands.
C. other women.
D. women themselves.
E. their desire for ease.

23.4
SIGNIFICANCE

The writer would undoubtedly be pleased if the reader would
A. support easier divorce laws.
B. become a non-conformist.
C. be broadminded enough to accept gigolos of either sex.
D. oppose economic discrimination against women.
E. refuse to take sides in the battle of the sexes.

23.6
APPLICATION

It is least probable that this passage was written during
A. 1945 - 1978.
B. 1925 - 1944.
C. 1900 - 1924.

D. 1875 - 1899.
E. a time prior to 1875.

23.7
TONE

In this passage the author looks on the plight of women with an attitude of
A. amusement.
B. indifference.
C. disapproval.

D. kindly indulgence.
E. condemnation.

The author protests that she is not a "feminist." By that she means that she
A. is interested in rights for people rather than for women.
B. is an essentially active person and cannot accept the role of passivity which society forces upon women.
C. is not feminine.
D. does not believe in equal social and economical rights for women.
E. is not a gigolo.

24

There exists an erroneous impression that methods of selection based on psychological tests are relatively new. This is almost certainly not true; stories of both sensible and absurd methods of selection can be found in the histories of many countries. Perhaps one of the oldest is to be found in the Bible, where Gideon is reported to have used a two-stage selection procedure in his war against the Midianites. The first method used was a kind of psychiatric screen based largely on reports of anxiety and depressive features. Apparently, a proclamation was read out to the effect that "Whosoever is fearful and afraid, let him return and depart early from Mount Gilead." The effect appears to have been quite remarkable because "there returned of the people twenty and two thousand; and there remained ten thousand."

This is a more severe reduction in numbers than would be tolerated by most modern commanders. However, Gideon went on to put into effect a second stage, consisting of a psychological performance test. This is most easily described by quoting from the Bible directly:

"And the Lord said unto Gideon, 'The people are yet too many; bring them down unto the water, and I will try them for thee there; and it shall be, that of whom I say unto thee, This shall go with thee, the same shall go with thee; and of whomsoever I say unto thee, This shall not go with thee, the same shall not go.'

So he brought down the people unto the water: and the Lord said unto Gideon, 'Everyone that lappeth of the water with his tongue, as a dog lappeth, him shalt thou set by himself; likewise every one that boweth down upon his knees to drink.'

"And the number of them that lapped, putting their hands to their mouth, were three hundred men; but all the rest of the people bowed down upon their knees to drink water.

And the Lord said unto Gideon, 'By the three hundred men that lapped will I save you, and deliver the Midianites into thine hand; and let all the other people go every man unto his place.' "

────────────── Questions for Passage #24 ──────────────

This passage centers about the
A. advantages of performance tests over psychiatric screening.
B. advantages of psychiatric screening over performance tests.
C. antiquity of psychological testing.
D. universality of cowardice.
E. universality of the Bible.

24.2
GENERALIZATION

Gideon's experience is referred to by the author to show that psychological testing

A. is useful.
B. has religious sanction.
C. is valid.
D. is not new.
E. must employ more than one form of test to get best results.

24.3
DETAIL

The group finally chosen by Gideon

A. bent their knees while drinking.
B. drank exactly as a dog would.
C. were chosen solely on the basis of their drinking habits.
D. preferred to fight the Midianites.
E. used their hands as cups.

24.5
CONCLUSION

In the second selection test the "bowing down on their knees to drink water" was probably interpreted by Gideon as a sign of

A. reverence.
B. weakness.
C. joy.
D. obedience.
E. fatigue.

25

Pete Hatsuoko had been born in this country, though one of his parents had been born in Japan. He went to the public schools and received a degree from the State University. He had never been to Japan. He could not read or write Japanese. He knew only a few Japanese phrases used in family small talk. After his induction into the Army, he was assigned to the Infantry. The orientation program included talks on the nature of the enemy. The captain in charge thought Pete should give one of the talks on "The Japanese Mentality." Pete tried in all candor to explain that he knew practically nothing about Japanese life and culture, that both his and his father's education had been received in this country. "But you're a Japanese," argued the Captain, "and you know about the Japanese. You prepare the talk." Pete did — from notes after he had read an Army handbook and a half-dozen popular magazine articles.

The evaluation of the two men may be analyzed as the **prototype** of a pattern which occurred frequently in the discussions. In a sense communication between them stopped when the conversation began. The issue was faced on quite different grounds by each. Pete oriented his thinking around facts. He talked in terms of them. He was, as far as is known, making statements which could have been verified or at least investigated. The Captain, on the other hand, seemed preoccupied with associations stirred up inside his nervous system by an accident of phrasing. The verbal classification *Japanese* received his attention so that Pete's talking was neglected. It was as if the label *Japanese* served as a stimulus pushing off the Captain's thinking in a direction removed from the situation. The direction can be plotted by his definition: "A Japanese is a person who knows about the Japanese. It follows, therefore, that Pete Hatsuoko is a person who knows about the Japanese. It follows, therefore, that Pete Hatsuoko can give the talk. Other factors in the situation need not be considered."

The Captain's misevaluations can be viewed as a response to his private verbal definition as if it were something more. The point being made is not that there is anything sinister in the Captain's private conjuring up of images. It is enough to note that the behavior which resulted was of a kind very different from that which would have taken account of the outside phenomena. Furthermore, decisions made on the basis of verbal associations, no matter how elaborate, are not the same as, nor commensurate with, those derived from consideration of facts. The point, in short, is this: evaluations based on the private elaboration of verbal formulae are not the same as, nor should they be equated with, evaluations based on verifiable descriptions or observations.

_____ Questions for Passage #25 _____

25.2
GENERALIZATION

Lack of communication between Hatsuoko and the army captain existed primarily because

A. the captain could not express himself easily.
B. the captain used verbal associations as a basis for action.
C. the captain did not like Japanese.
D. their ethnic backgrounds were different.
E. their ranks were so far apart.

25.5 (a)
CONCLUSION

The fact that Pete did not refuse to give the talk is

A. proof that the captain was right.
B. a reflection on his courage.
C. an implied criticism of the army.
D. a way of showing Pete's character.
E. a result of his lower military status.

25.5 (b)
CONCLUSION

The aspect of the concept "Japanese" which the captain neglected to take into account in evaluating Pete's suitability to give the talk was

A. cultural.   D. ethnic.
B. physiognomic.   E. patriotic.
C. decorative.

25.6
APPLICATION

It is a fact that most office buildings in the USA do not have a floor marked "13." If we accept the author's contention, we can conclude that

A. landlords have responded to a verbal concept as if it represented events in the real world.
B. landlords have previously had accidents happen to tenants on the thirteenth floors.
C. landlords follow custom.
D. landlords are probably not very intelligent.
E. by eliminating one number, namely "13," landlords can boast that their buildings are even taller than they really are.

25.7
TONE

In handling the subject of this passage, which involves a racial minority, the author is

A. scientifically detached.
B. apologetic for the army captain's treatment of Pete.
C. frustrated because of the impasse between the two men.
D. interested in showing the humor of Pete's making a talk from second-hand sources.
E. obviously for the "underdog."

25.8
VOCABULARY

The word "prototype" means

A. cause.   D. kind.
B. result.   E. modification.
C. model.

33

Communism has been successful wherever its tenets of social, economic, and political equality appeal to people for whom the removal of inequality has been the most urgent aspiration. Western philosophy has succeeded wherever in popular aspirations political liberty has taken precedence over all other needs. Thus Communism has largely lost the struggle for the minds of men in Central and Eastern Europe, and democracy has by and large been defeated in Asia. In Central and Eastern Europe the Communist promises of equality could not prevail against the life experiences the peoples of Central and Eastern Europe had with the tyranny of the Red Army and of the Russian secret police. In those regions, Communism had succeeded only with the segments of the population in whose life experiences the longing for equality, especially in the economic sphere, has taken precedence over the concern with liberty.

On the other hand, where democracy lost out in Asia it did so because its appeal was largely divorced from the life experiences and interests of the peoples of Asia. What the peoples of Asia want above everything else is freedom from Western colonialism. What chance was there for democracy to succeed in the struggle of ideas as long as democratic philosophy was contradicted by the life experiences of the peoples of Asia? The importance of political propaganda divorced from the life experiences of the common man is strikingly revealed in a report that appeared on September 30, 1950, in the *Chicago Daily News* under the by-line of Fred Sparks.

> The other day I visited a small farmer near Saigon . . . Through my interpreter I asked him to tell me what he thought of the Americans coming to Indochina. He said: "White men help white men. You give guns to help the French kill my people. We want to be rid of all foreigners and the Viet Minh . . . was slowly putting out the French."
>
> I said: "Don't you know there is a white man behind the Viet Minh? Don't you know that Ho Chi Minh takes Russian orders?"
>
> He said: "In Saigon I have seen Americans and I have seen Frenchmen. I have never heard of any white men being with the Viet Minh."

What makes this episode significant is the fact that to a large extent it is representative of Asia's reaction to Western ideas. Nowhere has this reaction been more drastic and more pregnant with dire consequences for the West than in China; for nowhere has the contrast between philosophy and the life experiences of the people been more drastic. The century-old anti-imperialistic record of the United States and the good will it had created in China for the United States were wiped out with one stroke when American weapons were used to kill Chinese and when American planes dropped bombs on the coastal cities of China. As a report in the London *Economist* put it with reference to the Nationalist air raids on Shanghai:

In the press these raids were presented as being quite as much the work of the "American Imperialists" as that of the "reactionary, remnant lackeys" of Taiwan, and while the raids drove out any faith in Chiang which might remain amongst the less educated, they no less effectively drove out any faith in America in quarters where it was still harboured.

————————————————— Questions for Passage #26 —————————————————

26.1
SUBJECT MATTER

A good title for this selection would be:

A. Why Communism Succeeds.

B. Why We Fail in Asia.

C. Why Democratic Ideology Fails.

D. Ideology and the Far East.

E. Why Communism and Democracy Succeed or Fail.

26.2
GENERALIZATION

According to the author, ideologies are most likely to fail if

A. the ideology comes in contact with a people who desire political liberty.

B. democratic and communistic ideologies come into conflict.

C. there is a discrepancy between the ideology and the life experience of the people.

D. the ideology comes in contact with a people beset by economic difficulties.

E. the ideology comes in contact with a people who do not desire equality.

26.3
DETAIL

America lost her long record of anti-imperialism because

A. the Asian press was against us.

B. the new Chinese nation was opposed to philosophy.

C. our propaganda appeal stressed political liberty rather than equality.

D. we acted like imperialists when we bombed Chinese cities.

E. we were associated with the losing side.

26.9
COMMUNICATION
TECHNIQUE

The author quotes a selection from the *Chicago Daily News* in order to

A. supply the reader with an enjoyable anecdote.

B. support his contention that democracy is losing the ideological warfare in the Far East.

C. support his contention that Asiatic people are staunch supporters of communistic ideas.

D. prove that criticism of western ideology is the result of the Asiatic's hatred of the white man.

E. support his contention that propaganda fails if divorced from the experience of the common people.

The nobler and more perfect a thing is, the later and slower it is in arriving at maturity. A man reaches the maturity of his reasoning powers and mental faculties hardly before the age of twenty-eight; a woman at eighteen. And then, too, in the case of woman, it is only reason of a sort — very niggard in its dimensions. That is why women remain children their whole life long; never seeing anything but what is quite close to them, cleaving to the present moment, taking appearance for reality, and preferring trifles to matters of the first importance. For it is by virtue of his reasoning faculty that man does not live in the present only, like the brute, but looks about him and considers the past and the future; and this is the origin of prudence, as well as of that care and anxiety which so many people exhibit. Both the advantages and the disadvantages which this involves, are shared in by the woman to a smaller extent because of her weaker power of reasoning. She may, in fact, be described as intellectually shortsighted, because, while she has an intuitive understanding of what lies quite close to her, her field of vision is narrow and does not reach to what is remote; so that things which are absent, or past, or to come, have much less effect upon women than upon men. This is the reason why women are more inclined to be extravagant, and sometimes carry their inclination to a length that borders upon madness. In their hearts, women think it is men's business to earn money and theirs to spend it — if possible during their husband's life, but, at any rate, after his death. The very fact that their husband hands them over his earnings for purposes of housekeeping, strengthens them in this belief.

However many disadvantages all this may involve, there is at least this to be said in its favor; that the woman lives more in the present than the man, and that, if the present is at all tolerable, she enjoys it more eagerly. This is the source of that cheerfulness which is peculiar to women, fitting her to amuse man in his hours of recreation, and, in case of need, to console him when he is borne down by the weight of his cares.

_____ Questions for Passage #27 _____

27.2 GENERALIZATION

According to the author, the major difference between a man's and a woman's intellect is that

A. men mature much later than women.
B. men have a broader view of things.
C. women are more cheerful than men.
D. man's intellect is nobler than that of woman.
E. women are frivolous and extravagant.

27.3 DETAIL

The cause of women's frivolity and cheerfulness is that

A. men do not challenge their intellect.
B. they are irresponsible by their very nature.
C. they live more in the present.
D. they want to console men.
E. they reach maturity too fast.

27.6
APPLICATION

The author is probably a

A. philosopher.   D. biologist.

B. gossip columnist.   E. communist.

C. happily married man.

27.7
TONE

The author's attitude toward women can best be described as

A. contemptuous.   D. cynical.

B. condescending.   E. pitying.

C. paternal.

28

Fried foods have long been frowned upon. Nevertheless, the skillet is about our handiest and most useful piece of kitchen equipment. Stalwart lumberjacks and others engaged in active labor requiring 4,000 calories per day or more will take approximately one-third of their rations prepared in this fashion. Meat, eggs, and French toast cooked in this way are served in millions of homes daily. Apparently the consumers are not beset with more signs of indigestion than afflict those who insist upon broiling, roasting, or boiling. Some years ago one of our most eminent physiologists investigated the digestibility of fried potatoes. He found that the pan variety was more easily broken down for assimilation than when deep fat was employed. The latter, however, dissolved within the alimentary tract more readily than the boiled type. Furthermore, he learned, by watching the progress of the contents of the stomach by means of the fluoroscope, that fat actually accelerated the rate of digestion. Now all this is quite in contrast with "authority." Volumes have been written on nutrition, and everywhere the dictum has been accepted — no fried edibles of any sort for children. A few will go so far as to forbid this style of cooking wholly. Now and then an expert will be bold enough to admit that he uses them himself, the absence of discomfort being explained on the ground that he possesses a powerful gastric apparatus. We can of course sizzle perfectly good articles to death so that they will be leathery and tough. But thorough heating, in the presence of shortening, is not the awful crime that it has been labeled. Such dishes stimulate rather than retard contractions of the gall bladder. Thus it is that bile mixes with the nutriment shortly after it leaves the stomach. We don't need to allow our foodstuffs to become oil soaked, but other than that, there seems to be no basis for the widely heralded prohibition against this method. But notions become fixed. The first condemnation probably arose because an "oracle" suffered from dyspepsia which he ascribed to some fried item on the menu. The theory spread. Others agreed with him, and after a time the doctrine became incorporated in our textbooks. The belief is now tradition rather than proved fact. It should have been refuted long since, as experience has demonstrated its falsity.

Go on to next page. ➤

28.1
SUBJECT MATTER

This passage focuses on
A. why the skillet is a handy piece of kitchen equipment.
B. the digestibility of fried foods.
C. how the experts can mislead the public in the area of food preparation.
D. why fried foods have long been frowned upon.
E. methods of preparing foods.

28.2
GENERALIZATION

The author's main idea is that
A. fried foods have long been frowned upon.
B. contrary to popular opinion, fried foods are more easily assimilated than boiled foods.
C. fried foods are more easily digested than boiled or broiled foods though many authorities believe the opposite to be true.
D. the public should eat more fried foods since they are as easily digested as boiled foods.
E. despite the traditional condemnation of fried foods, they are as easily digested as foods cooked in other ways.

28.3
DETAIL

Apparently much fried food is eaten because
A. it is easily prepared.
B. people engaged in active labor need the calories that fat supplies.
C. it is healthful.
D. it is easily digested.
E. people do not read about nutrition.

28.4
SIGNIFICANCE

The author strongly implies that the public should
A. avoid fried foods if possible.
B. prepare some foods by frying.
C. fry foods intended for adults but not for children.
D. prepare all foods by frying.
E. avoid deep fat frying but otherwise fry selected foods.

28.7
TONE

When the author says that an "oracle suffered from dyspepsia which he ascribed to some fried item on the menu" he is being
A. bitter.   D. inventive.
B. factual.   E. sarcastic.
C. humorous.

28.9
COMMUNICATION
TECHNIQUE

The selection was probably taken from
A. a medical journal.
B. a publication addressed to the general public.
C. a speech at a medical convention.
D. an advertisement for cooking oil.
E. a laboratory report.

29

All museum adepts are acquainted with examples of *ostrakoi,* the oyster shells used in balloting. As a matter of fact, these "oyster shells" are usually shards of pottery, conveniently glazed to enable the voter to express his wishes in writing. In the Agora a great number of these have come to light, bearing the thrilling name, Themistocles. Into rival jars were dropped the ballots for or against his banishment. On account of the huge vote taken on that memorable day, it was to be expected that many ostrakoi would be found, but the interest of this collection is that a number of these ballots are inscribed in an *identical* handwriting. There is nothing mysterious about it! The Boss was on the job, then as now. He prepared these ballots and voters cast them — no doubt for the consideration of an **obol** or two. *The ballot box was stuffed.*

How is the glory of the American boss diminished! A vile imitation, he. His methods as old as Time!

—————————————— Questions for Passage #29 ——————————————

29.1
SUBJECT MATTER

The title that best expresses the theme of this passage is
A. Democracy in the Past.
B. An Odd Method of Voting.
C. Themistocles, An Early Dictator.
D. The Boss's Role in Elections — Today and Yesterday.
E. The Vanishing American Politician.

29.4
SIGNIFICANCE

The author would apparently want the reader to
A. take a stand against Bossism.
B. regard the American Boss in historical perspective.
C. become familiar with archeological discoveries.
D. feel angry about Themistocles' unjust banishment.
E. be suspicious about elections.

29.5
CONCLUSION

The author suggests that the verdict against Themistocles was to a certain extent
A. justified.
B. mysterious.
C. predetermined.
D. unpopular.
E. unimportant.

29.6
APPLICATION

One of the characteristic methods of a political Boss involves gifts to constituents of his district at Christmas time. If the author's conclusion about Bosses is correct, such a tactic would be similar in purpose to
A. the institution of "ombudsman" — an official in Scandinavian lands whose function it is to represent the citizens to the officials.
B. the appointment by the City of Athens of an officer whose sole duty it was to watch that city officials did not steal from the public treasury.
C. the distribution of "bread and circuses" to the Roman poor by Roman rulers to gain the people's favor.
D. the rewarding of spies in Roman times with portions of the "traitor's" estate.
E. none of the above.

29.7
TONE

The tone of the second paragraph of the passage is
A. self-righteous.
B. sarcastic.
C. insincere.
D. matter-of-fact.
E. mildly cynical.

29.8
VOCABULARY

An "obol," as used in the passage, is evidently
A. a Greek coin.
B. a promise of bread.
C. a complimentary remark.
D. an appointive public office.
E. an oyster shell.

Fire can be thought of as any combustion process intense enough to emit light. It may be a quietly burning flame or the brilliant flash of an explosion.

A typical combustion process is the burning of gasoline in an automobile engine. The vaporized fuel is mixed with air, compressed in the engine's cylinder, and ignited by a spark. As the fuel flames up, the heat produced flows into the adjacent layer of unburned fuel and ignites it. In this way a zone of fire spreads throughout the fuel mixture until the combustion is complete. This moving zone of burning fuel is called a combustion wave.

The speed at which such a combustion wave travels through a fuel mixture is called the burning velocity of the mixture. The burning velocity of a gas such as methane quietly burning in air is only about one foot per second. By comparison, the burning velocity of more reactive combinations such as the rocket fuels, hydrogen and fluorine, can be hundreds of feet per second.

If the fuel flows at the same speed as the combustion wave, the result is a stationary flame, like the one in your kitchen gas burner. In the kitchen burner a jet of gas mixed with air flows from the openings in the head of the burner. If the velocity of the fuel mixture flowing from the opening is greater than its burning velocity, the flame blows out.

In jet engines speeding through the air at 500 to 600 miles per hour, the engine's flame is sometimes blown out by the blast of air entering the combustion chamber at high speeds. Jet pilots call this condition "flameout."

Combustion can sometimes occur very slowly. A familiar example of slow combustion is the drying of ordinary oil-based paint. In this chemical reaction, called *oxidation*, the oxygen in the air reacts with the drying oil in the paint to provide a tough film. The linseed oil molecules link together, forming an insoluble coating. Another example is the hardening and cracking of rubber with age. One way to avoid this is to incorporate certain chemicals called inhibitors into the compound.

How can the chemical reaction involved in such a quiet process as the drying of paint also produce spectacular flames and explosions? The main difference between the two is the temperature at which they occur.

At lower temperatures the reaction must take place over a long time. The heat which is slowly produced is dissipated to the surroundings and does not speed up the reaction. When the heat produced by the low-temperature reaction is retained instead of being dissipated, the system breaks into flame. This is the process that accounts for a major fire hazard, spontaneous combustion, as when oily rags suddenly burst into flame.

In a flame or explosion, the reactions are extremely fast. In many chemical processes, however, such a rapid oxidation process would be extremely destructive.

30.2
GENERALIZATION

The major difference between *oxidation* and *fire* is that
A. their burning velocities differ in rate.
B. oxidation is a chemical reaction while fire is a physical reaction.
C. oxidation does not create heat.
D. they occur at different temperatures.
E. none of the above are true.

30.3 (a)
DETAIL

Rocket fuels are more explosive than methane gas because of
A. the temperature at which combustion takes place.
B. the degree of oxidation accomplished by the combustion process.
C. the presence of inhibitors.
D. the location of the combustion.
E. the greater burning velocity.

30.3 (b)
DETAIL

A steady flame in a gas range is the result of
A. a burning velocity equal to the combustion wave.
B. fuel being supplied at the same rate as the combustion wave.
C. fuel being supplied at a higher rate than that of the burning velocity.
D. a free-flowing supply of air from the openings in the head of the burner.
E. a low combustion wave.

30.6
APPLICATION

Which of the following could *not* be defined as combustion?
A. a quietly burning flame.
B. an explosion.
C. a radiator giving off heat.
D. the drying of oil-based paint.
E. the action of a diesel motor.

30.7
TONE

An attempt on the part of the author of this passage to give a more informal tone to his writing occurs in
A. paragraph 2.   D. paragraph 7.
B. paragraph 4.   E. paragraphs 5 and 7.
C. paragraph 5.

31

The energy which the sun radiates goes in every direction, and only a minute part of it falls on the earth. Even so, it represents power of approximately 5,000,000 horsepower per square mile per day; the sun gives us as much energy every minute as mankind utilizes in a year. At present, we use this energy indirectly, and it is our only final source of power. Coal represents the chemical action of the sun on green plants thousands of years ago. Water power results from the sun's creating vapor and subsequent rain. Even windmills operate because of air currents set in motion by the different heating effects of the sun in different places. Some day, through chemistry or some type of solar motor, we shall harness this titanic source of energy more directly. Already, a scientist has worked out an engine, surprisingly efficient, in which the sun's rays are concentrated through mirrors on a tube of water to create steam.

Go on to next page. ➤

31.1
SUBJECT MATTER

In this passage the author discusses primarily
A. our ultimate source of power.
B. solar chemistry.
C. the amount of solar radiation.
D. how water power is produced.
E. harnessing energy through chemistry.

31.3
DETAIL

The extent to which mankind utilizes solar energy available is approximately
A. 5%.   D. 50%.
B. 100%, but indirectly.   E. 1,000%.
C. less than 1%.

31.5
CONCLUSION

Man cannot utilize all the solar energy falling on the earth because
A. only a minute part of the solar energy reaches the earth.
B. the sun produces different heating effects in different places.
C. it takes thousands of years for the formation of coal deposits.
D. the sun is too distant from the earth.
E. scientific knowledge is insufficient.

31.9
COMMUNICATION
TECHNIQUE

Select the statement which is a supporting DETAIL rather than a GENERALIZATION.
A. The sun is our final source of power.
B. The fraction of the sun's energy which we use is used indirectly.
C. Man uses only a tiny portion of the sun's energy.
D. Already one device using solar energy directly has been developed.
E. Some day we will use the sun's energy directly.

32

It is **curious** to note how slowly the mechanism of the intellectual life improves. Contrast the ordinary library facilities of a middle-class English home, such as the present writer is now working in, with the inconveniences and deficiencies of the equipment of an Alexandrian writer, and one realizes the enormous waste of time, physical exertion, and attention that went on through all the centuries during which that library flourished. Before the present writer lie half a dozen books, and there are good indices to three of them. He can pick up any one of these six books, refer quickly to a statement, verify a quotation, and go on writing. Contrast with that the tedious unfolding of a rolled manuscript. Close at hand are two encyclopedias, a dictionary, an atlas of the world, a biographical dictionary, and other books of reference. They have no marginal indices, it is true; but that, perhaps, is asking too much at present. There were no such resources in the world in 300 B.C. Alexandria had still to produce the first grammar and the first dictionary. This present book is being written in manuscript; it is then taken by a typist and typewritten very accurately. It can then, with the utmost convenience, be read over, corrected amply, rearranged freely, retyped, and recorrected. The Alexandrian author had to dictate or recopy every word he wrote. Before he could turn back to what he had written previously, he had to dry his last words by waving them in the air or pouring sand over them; he had not even blotting-paper. Whatever an author wrote had to be recopied again and again before it could reach any considerable circle of readers, and every copyist introduced some new error. New books were dictated to a roomful of copyists, and so issued in a first edition of some hundreds at least. In Rome, Horace and Virgil seem to have been issued in quite considerable editions. Whenever a need for maps or diagrams arose, there were fresh difficulties. Such a science as anatomy, for example, depending as it does upon accurate drawing, must have been enormously hampered by the natural limitations of the copyist. The transmission of geographical fact again must have been almost incredibly tedious. No doubt a day will come when a private library and writing desk of the year A.D. 1925 will seem quaintly clumsy and difficult; but, measured by the standards of Alexandria, they are astonishly quick, efficient, and economical of nervous and mental energy.

_____ Questions for Passage #32 _____

32.1
SUBJECT MATTER

The best title for this passage might be
A. The Difficulties of Alexandrian Writers.
B. The Advance of Writing and Publishing Since Alexandrian Times.
C. The Advantages of Present Day (1925 A.D.) Writers.
D. The Inadequacies of Ancient and Modern Times.
E. none of the above.

32.3
DETAIL

According to this passage, books written in Alexandria were
A. each produced one at a time.
B. produced with excellent maps and diagrams because of the care expended upon them by copyists.
C. necessarily produced by dictation.
D. severely limited in output because of technical difficulties.
E. blotted as each page was written.

32.7
TONE

In writing about his subject, the writer apparently
A. wants to share his interests in his discoveries about the intellectual life with his reader.
B. gloats over the difficulties of ancient writers.
C. slyly introduces the fact that he is economically secure.
D. is a practical historian who sticks to established facts.
E. is impatient with the improvements that have been made in a writer's tools.

32.8
VOCABULARY

The author used the word "curious" to mean
A. strange.   D. interesting.
B. inquisitive.   E. none of the above.
C. scholarly.

32.9 (a)
COMMUNICATION TECHNIQUE

In developing his case about writing, past and and present, the author makes use primarily of
A. incident.   D. analogy.
B. comparison.   E. contrast.
C. deductive reasoning.

32.9 (b)
COMMUNICATION TECHNIQUE

The first sentence of this passage
A. is another way of expressing the main thought of the passage.
B. is supported by the remainder of the passage.
C. appears to contradict the main thought of the passage.
D. has no connection with the passage.
E. appears to have little connection with the rest of the passage.

Never amidst the clamors of the college where I passed so many days, months, years, did I ever hear a single word about the application of logic. I had faith then (the scholar ought to have faith, according to Aristotle) that it was not necessary to trouble myself about what logic is and what its purpose is, but that it concerned itself solely with creating a motive for our clamors and our disputes. I therefore disputed and clamored with all my might. If I were defending in a class a thesis **according to the categories**, I believed it my duty never to yield to my opponent, were he one hundred times right, but to seek some very subtle distinction, in order to obscure the whole issue. On the other hand, were I disputant, all my care and efforts tended not to enlighten my opponent, but to beat him by some argument, good or bad: even so had I been taught and directed. The categories of Aristotle were like a ball that we give to children to play with, and that it was necessary to get back by our clamors when we had lost it. If, on the other hand, we should get it, we should not through any outcry allow it to be recovered. I was then persuaded that all **dialectic** reduced itself to disputing with loud and vigorous cries.

———————————————— Questions for Passage #33 ————————————————

33.3
DETAIL

The author tells us how he used to argue at college in his youth. One of the methods he did *not* use was
A. avoidance of the issues.
B. clamor.
C. judicious reasoning.
D. quibbling.
E. stubbornness.

33.5
CONCLUSION

The author appears to be
A. opposed to logic.
B. an undergraduate.
C. enthusiastic about Aristotle's wisdom.
D. more reflective than when he went to college.
E. opposed to the pursuit of scholarship.

33.7
TONE

The author looks back on his college days with
A. adverse criticism.
B. violent distaste.
C. approval.
D. bitterness.
E. pleasure.

33.8 (a)
VOCABULARY

By stating that he defended a thesis "according to the categories," the author means that
A. he defended a thesis logically.
B. he applied certain formal steps in logic to whatever the subject was.
C. he took whatever side was assigned to him.
D. he denied his opponent the right to speak by shouting him down.
E. he refused to listen to his opponent.

33.8 (b)
VOCABULARY

By "dialectic" the author means
A. caustic remarks.
B. slang.
C. debating.
D. athletic contests.
E. speaking quaintly.

There are a few books which go with midnight, solitude, and a candle. It is much easier to say what does not please us then than what is exactly right. The book must be, anyhow, something benedictory by a sinning fellow man. Cleverness would be repellent at such an hour. Cleverness, anyhow, is the level of mediocrity today; we are all too infernally clever. The first witty and perverse paradox blows out the candle. Only the sick mind craves cleverness, as a morbid body turns to drink. The late **candle** throws its beams a great distance; and its rays make transparent much that seemed massy and important. The mind at rest beside that light, when the house is asleep, and the consequential affairs of the urgent world have diminished to their right proportions because we see them distantly from another and a more tranquil place in the heavens, where duty, honor, silly arguments, controversial logic on great questions, appear such as will leave hardly a trace of fossil in the indurated mud which will cover them — the mind then smiles at cleverness. For though at that hour the body may be dog-tired, the mind is white and lucid, like that of a man from whom a fever has abated. It is bare of illusions. It has a sharp focus, small and starlike, as a clear and lonely flame left burning by the altar of a shrine from which all have gone but one. A book which approaches that light in the privacy of that place must come, as it were, with open and honest pages.

—————————————— Questions for Passage #34 ——————————————

34.7
TONE

A reading of this passage would indicate that its author is a person who is most probably
A. anxious to please.
B. serious.
C. up-to-date.
D. paradoxical and witty.
E. unforgiving.

34.8
VOCABULARY

By "candle" the author refers to
A. study in the late night.
B. clear analysis of books.
C. the clear mind seeking truth.
D. a light-giving source.
E. a clear and lonely flame at an altar.

34.9
COMMUNICATION
TECHNIQUE

In defining the type of book he prefers at midnight, the author
A. presents negative arguments exclusively.
B. presents his arguments with full self-confidence that he can arrive at a clear definition.
C. adheres to conventional literary values.
D. presents both negative and positive factors for judging a book.
E. cites specific examples of books which meet his criteria.

The relation of the sales tax to the problem of social balance is admirably direct. The community is affluent in privately produced goods. It is poor in public services. The obvious solution is to tax the former to provide the latter — by making private goods more expensive, public goods are made more abundant. Motion pictures, electronic equipment, and cigarettes are made more costly so that schools can be more handsomely supported. We pay more for soap, detergents, and vacuum cleaners in order that we may have cleaner cities and less occasion to use them. We have more expensive cars and gasoline so that we may have highways and streets on which to drive them. Food being comparatively cheap and abundant, we tax it in order to have better medical services and better health in which to enjoy it. This forthright solution has the further advantage that sales taxation can be employed with fair efficiency by states and even by cities. It is in the services rendered by these governments that the problem of social balance is especially severe. The yield of the sales tax increases with increasing production. As wants are contrived for private goods, more revenues are provided for public use. The general property tax, the principal alternative to the sales tax, is rigid and inflexible. Since its rates must ordinarily be raised for additional services, including those that are associated with increasing income and product, the burden of proving need is especially heavy. This tax is a poor servant of social balance.

─────────────── Questions for Passage #35 ───────────────

35.3
DETAIL

One reason the author cites for not regarding the property tax as an ideal solution to social needs is that
A. it must be changed by law.
B. each rise in rates must depend on establishing the need for additional services.
C. it can be imposed by cities but not by states.
D. since the community is not wealthy in property and homes, little can be spared from property income in taxes.
E. it is not forthright, as is the sales tax.

35.5
CONCLUSION

The author feels that the *chief* advantage of the sales tax is that it
A. is easy to administer.
B. is applicable to wide areas.
C. can be imposed by cities and states.
D. is a direct means of achieving social balance.
E. is less punitive than the property tax.

35.6
APPLICATION

New York City is faced with the need for additional funds to provide services to its inhabitants. The author would most probabaly advise the mayor to
A. discourage consumption of goods.
B. raise the property tax.
C. increase the prices of private goods.
D. find an alternative to sales and property taxes.
E. raise the (existing) sales tax.

The focusing or sharpening of the image is performed by a special apparatus. In every camera, the farther the object is from the eye, the farther forward — and the nearer the object is to the eye, the farther backward — is its image thrown. In photographers' cameras the back is made to slide, and can be drawn away from the lens when the object that casts the picture is near, and pushed forward when it is far. The picture is thus kept always sharp. But no such change of length is possible in the eyeball; and the same result is reached in another way. The lens, namely, grows more convex when a near object is looked at, and flatter when the object recedes. This change is due to the antagonism of the "ciliary muscle." The ligament, when the ciliary muscle is at rest, assumes such a spread-out shape as to keep the lens rather flat. But the lens is highly elastic; and it springs into the more convex form which is natural to it whenever the ciliary muscle, by contracting, causes the ligament to relax its pressure. The contraction of the muscle, by thus rendering the lens more refractive, adapts the eye for near objects ("accommodates" it for them, as we say): and its relaxation, by rendering the lens less refractive, adapts the eye for distant vision. Accommodation for the near is thus the more *active* change, since it involves contraction of the ciliary muscle. When we look far off, we simply let our eyes go passive. We feel the difference in the effort when we compare the two sensations of change.

Questions for Passage #36

36.2 GENERALIZATION

In order to focus on distant objects, the lens of the eye
A. becomes more convex.
B. becomes more active.
C. becomes more refractive.
D. contracts the ciliary muscle.
E. flattens.

36.3 DETAIL

The ligament, when not acted on by the contraction of the ciliary muscle,
A. maintains its pressure on the lens so that the lens remains flat.
B. relaxes its pressure on the lens so that it remains convex.
C. maintains a pressure on the lens so that the lens remains convex.
D. relaxes its pressure on the lens so that it remains flat.
E. does not influence the lens in any of the above ways.

36.5 CONCLUSION

Functionally, we may compare
A. the lens of the camera with the lens of the eye.
B. the lens of the camera with the ciliary muscle.
C. the lens of the eye with the sliding of the back of the camera.
D. the sliding of the back of the camera with the adaptability of the eyeball.
E. the ciliary muscle with the eye ligament.

36.6 APPLICATION

Which of the following activities is most tiring for the lens of the eye?
A. looking at a distant mountain
B. being a "sidewalk superintendent"
C. watching squirrels being fed
D. reading a book
E. watching a movie

36.7 TONE

The tone of this passage can best be described as
A. professionally scientific.
B. argumentative.
C. matter of fact and formal.
D. informal and matter of fact.
E. being none of the above.

Tests conducted at the University of Pennsylvania's Psychological Laboratory showed that anger is one of the most difficult emotions to detect from facial expression. Professor Dallas E. Buzby confronted 716 students with pictures of extremely angry persons, and asked them to identify the emotion from the facial expression. Only two percent made correct judgments. Anger was most frequently judged as "pleased." And a typical reaction of a student confronted with the picture of a man who was hopping mad was to classify his expression as either "bewildered," "quizzical," or simply "amazed." Other studies showed that it is extremely difficult to tell whether a man is angry or not just by looking at his face. The investigators found further that women are better at detecting anger from facial expression than men are. **Paradoxically**, they found that psychological training does not sharpen one's ability to judge a man's emotions by his expressions but appears actually to hinder it. For in the university tests, the more courses the subject had taken in psychology, the poorer judgment scores he turned in.

———————————————— Questions for Passage #37 ————————————————

37.1
SUBJECT MATTER

The information in this passage centers about
A. the relation between anger and other emotions.
B. the findings of Professor Dallas E. Buzby.
C. the differences between men and women with respect to emotion.
D. the influence of psychology on perceptiveness.
E. the detection of anger from facial expression.

37.2
GENERALIZATION

The main thought of this passage is that anger
A. is difficult to detect by looking at a person's face.
B. is frequently confused with other emotions.
C. is detected by women better than by men.
D. cannot be detected by a psychologically trained person.
E. is akin to bewilderment in its effects.

37.3
DETAIL

Students with psychological training who were tested
A. marked less than two percent of their possible choices correctly.
B. were less able to judge correctly than the average student.
C. did better than the average student in the group.
D. did as well as the women students.
E. performed in a manner not specified.

37.5
CONCLUSION

To achieve the greatest success in detecting anger from facial expression, it would be best to
A. use adults rather than students as judges.
B. ask women in fields other than psychology to judge.
C. ask women rather than men to judge.
D. ask psychologists to judge.
E. be satisfied with a two percent success, if such a percentage was guaranteed.

37.8
VOCABULARY
The author uses the word "paradoxically" in his sentence about psychological training to imply that
A. we can expect such training to have the effect stated.
B. we should expect such training to result in better scores.
C. such information is offered as an afterthought.
D. such information is an interesting sidelight of the findings.
E. such information is true of other kinds of training as well.

38

There are millions of pain nerves in the body, and when any of them are even slighty disturbed, they flash a pain impulse to the brain. The brain weighs this message, evaluates it in terms of so much pain or discomfort. When a state of tension exists, it causes the brain to overvalue pain impulses — thus causing you to feel far more uncomfortable than you otherwise would. On the other hand, when you are relaxed, pain messages tend to be evaluated on a much lower scale. Tests show that up to 75 percent of the pain (or disagreeable sensation) which exists when a person is tense vanishes entirely when he relaxes.

──────────────── Questions for Passage #38 ────────────────

38.1
SUBJECT MATTER
The author of this passage is most interested in telling us about
A. a simple formula for happiness.
B. the way the pain nerves work.
C. the results of tests carried out on tense persons.
D. the relationship of the brain to pain feelings.
E. the effect of tension on comfort or discomfort.

38.2
GENERALIZATION
The main idea of the passage is that
A. if you fly off the handle easily, try to learn to relax.
B. the brain evaluates a pain impulse in accordance with the degree of tension in the body.
C. the brain evaluates each pain signal in terms of so much pain or discomfort.
D. tests show that up to 75% of pain which exists when a person is tense vanishes when he relaxes.
E. the millions of pain nerves in the body are each able to flash a pain message to the brain when even slightly disturbed.

38.4
SIGNIFICANCE
To reduce pain, it would probably be best to
A. build up tension in your body.
B. learn to relax.
C. evaluate pain messages on a lower scale.
D. increase your sense of mental well-being.
E. do none of the above.

38.5
CONCLUSION
We can conclude from the passage that a person's feeling of discomfort
A. is the result of bodily states beyond his control.
B. is controlled by his brain and thus is beyond his influence.
C. is influenced by his mental and emotional state.
D. is usually minor and can be ignored.
E. depends on how the individual evaluates it.

Though the pain from a scorpion's sting is intense and may endure for several hours, there is little danger of serious and lasting injury. The scorpion is a sinister-looking creature, with an armored, segmented body supported by eight legs. It possesses numerous eyes, yet for all practical purposes it is devoid of vision, with only monstrous, finger-like pincers to guide it. These oversized pincers are powerful weapons with which the scorpion seizes and crushes its prey. The jointed tail, with its poison needle point, can be wielded with deadly accuracy if the pincers are not effective. Sinister as is the scorpion in the insect world, there is no reason why it should be feared by man. Its enemies are principally insects that destroy grain fields, and in killing these pests the scorpion serves a beneficent purpose.

_____ Questions for Passage #39 _____

**39.1
SUBJECT MATTER**

A title for this passage might be
A. Insects to Know and Love.
B. A Forbidding Ally.
C. The Scorpion — Man's Best Friend.
D. Enemies of the Scorpion.
E. The Scorpion's Sting.

**39.2
GENERALIZATION**

The passage definitely states that the scorpion
A. is completely blind.
B. is harmless.
C. is useful to man.
D. is pleasant looking.
E. lives on a diet consisting solely of insects harmful to man.

**39.4
SIGNIFICANCE**

The author suggests that the reader need not
A. avoid scorpions.
B. know about scorpions.
C. disarm scorpions.
D. breed scorpions.
E. fear scorpions.

**39.5
CONCLUSION**

The scorpion's primary threat to its enemies lies in its
A. pincers.
B. speed of motion.
C. armored body.
D. pointed tail.
E. range of vision.

**39.8
VOCABULARY**

"Montrous," as used in the passage, means
A. sinister.
B. powerful.
C. deformed.
D. large.
E. unconcealed.

Franklin D. Roosevelt collected stamps, welcomed Boy Scouts, rode in an open car down Pennsylvania Avenue on state occasions, and traveled to far-distant lands for weighty **confabulations** with heads of state. In these ways he was not unique. In one way only he differed from his contemporaries and from his predecessors. He had high regard for the popular consensus. When Congress fought him on the so-called "packing of the Supreme Court," he didn't call in the Democratic whips for a tongue-lashing, he went on the radio. And when critics inside and outside Congress accused his New Deal of being a concoction of "alphabet soup," he didn't upbraid Congress or send them messages; he scheduled another fireside chat.

_____ Questions for Passage #40 _____

40.1
SUBJECT MATTER

This selection can best be titled
A. F. D. R.
B. Congress and F. D. R.
C. F. D. R.'s Strategy.
D. F. D. R., Radio Personality.
E. The Varied Interests of F. D. R.

40.2
GENERALIZATION

The best statement of the main idea of this passage is that F. D. R.
A. liked to make public speeches.
B. used party control to pressure congressmen.
C. carried on a large variety of activities while President.
D. relied on the people as his source of power.
E. was a unique President.

40.3
DETAIL

F. D. R. scheduled "fireside chats"
A. because he had an outgoing personality.
B. to avoid antagonizing his party lieutenants.
C. because, like many people in the public eye, he had a bit of the "ham" in him.
D. because drafting messages to Congress bored him.
E. to swing public opinion to his support.

40.7
TONE

The author's attitude toward F. D. R. is
A. critical.
B. matter of fact.
C. humorous.
D. approving.
E. sarcastic.

40.8
VOCABULARY

"Confabulations," as used in the passage, means
A. parliamentary meetings.
B. social visits.
C. military reviews.
D. bargaining sessions involving deception.
E. exchange of views.

Civil aeronautics authorities argue that modern aviation has rendered the Mercator projection map of the world, which places the globe on a flat surface, entirely out of place. Polar regions, which have been practically ignored on the map, now become very important. The flying of the future will be in the stratosphere, and this flying can be done more easily in the polar regions than elsewhere. The Arctic Ocean will not in the future be a barrier to commercial and war planes as in the past, but an avenue easily accessible. If one flies northward from the United States to the North Pole and keeps on flying, he will soon find himself in Siberia. The new geography also teaches that if the Japanese were to fly by the most direct route from Tokyo to Panama, they would pass over Denver. Minneapolis is 300 miles nearer to Tokyo than is San Diego. Madison, Wisconsin, is nearer to the most distant capital of Europe than to any of the large South American cities.

_____Questions for Passages #41_____

41.1
SUBJECT MATTER

A good title for this passage might be
A. The Importance of Geographical Knowledge.
B. Future Traveling in the Arctic Regions.
C. Interesting Geographic Facts.
D. Flying in the Stratosphere.
E. How Geography is Affected by Stratospheric Flying.

41.3
DETAIL

Madison, Wisconsin, is nearer to Berlin than it is to
A. Denver.
B. Rio de Janeiro.
C. New York.
D. Nome.
E. San Diego.

41.5
CONCLUSION

The Mercator projection is inadequate because it
A. is too small.
B. does not show the stratosphere.
C. is too old.
D. does not show air distances correctly.
E. does not show Siberia.

41.6
APPLICATION

Based on the information in this passage, the best location for defensive warning installations against possible air attack from the Soviet Union would be
A. along the Gulf Coast and the Rio Grande.
B. along the Eastern seaboard.
C. along the Pacific coast.
D. on seadromes in the Eastern Atlantic Ocean.
E. in Northern Canada.

42

The research department of Booz, Allen, and Hamilton has been analyzing the attitudes of some 422 executives who have changed jobs. The findings appear to come together on one vital point: in the majority of cases the primary reason for switching was not money, increased security, or location. The executives switched most often because advancement was blocked. With executives checking only one reason for switching, the order was: (1) bigger job, more responsibility; (2) don't like present management policies; (3) advancement in company uncertain; (4) change of activity desired. In seventh place: increased income. It is clear between the lines that the great motivating factor was the sense of a ceiling, psychological or actual, in one job and the need for more self-expression through another. Security is rarely mentioned.

———————————— Questions for Passage #42 ————————————

42.1
SUBJECT MATTER

This passage centers about

A. why executive positions are hard to fill.

B. the role of security in executives' motivation.

C. what executives seek in a job.

D. the work of Booz, Allen, and Hamilton.

E. the need to examine data obtained on questionnaires to determine their true implications.

42.2
GENERALIZATION

The main idea of this passage is that

A. it was necessary to read "between the lines" to find out what executives really thought about their jobs.

B. the reasons given by 422 executives who switched jobs were (1) bigger job, more responsibility, (2) don't like present management policies, (3) advancement in company uncertain, (4) change of activity desired, in that order.

C. since executives who were surveyed checked only one reason, the results of the survey were too simple to be a true indication of why most of them switched.

D. executives changed jobs because advancement was blocked.

E. according to Booz, Allen, and Hamilton, most executives who were surveyed were not interested in money or security.

42.3
DETAIL

A reason *not* among those cited as being among the secondary factors causing executives to change was

A. larger salary

B. more security.

C. bigger job.

D. better location.

E. a factor not specified in in the passage.

42.5
CONCLUSION

We can reasonably conclude from this passage that

A. executives are pretty much like most people who work.

B. Booz, Allen, and Hamilton did not have a specific reason in mind for conducting the research.

C. the findings do not justify the researchers' conclusions about executives.

D. executives as a group have at least one personal characteristic in common.

E. the executives as a whole falsified their attitude toward money.

42.9
COMMUNICATION TECHNIQUE

In discussing the agency's research, the author

A. presents the agency's findings and conclusions.

B. omits the specific breakdown of data found but states the agency's conclusions.

C. seems confused by the lack of emphasis on the security factor.

D. draws conclusions that appear sound but are not sufficiently established by the data presented.

E. presents the findings and lets the reader draw his own conclusions.

To the visitor from the hinterland who lands in midtown Manhattan, the impression is one of confusion, noise, dirt, and monumental indifference. "Is this," he asks, "the celebrated Mecca that annually draws businessmen, students, job-seekers, and tourists from every corner of the globe?" If he swiftly decides that "It's a nice place to visit, but . . . ," he has failed to find New York's **open sesame**. The jade expert can find an emperor's collection of carvings in the Jade Room of the Metropolitan Museum of Art. The artist can leisurely study a rare volume of William Blake's etchings in one of the specialized rooms of the Main Library, or walk for years through the endless public and private galleries. The chess player finds his friends at the Marshall Chess Club, the tired businessman his excitement at the Copa, the historian his archives at the Butler Library, the Orientalist his confreres at Asia House. But New York's magic door will open only if the visitor arrives with a key.

Questions for Passage #43

43.2 GENERALIZATION

The best title summing up this passage is
A. New York Recipe: Seekers Shall Be Finders.
B. Why New York Is Disappointing.
C. Places to See in the Big City.
D. New York, Something for Everybody.
E. New York, Haven for the Gifted.

43.4 SIGNIFICANCE

The passage would have the prospective visitor to New York
A. come with an open mind.
B. postpone judgment.
C. come with some specific interest.
D. ask for a key to the city.
E. try to see all the attractions before leaving.

43.5 CONCLUSION

The author's purpose in writing the passage is to
A. show his knowledge of New York.
B. defend the reputation of New York.
C. publicize some of New York's tourist attractions.
D. help "out-of-towners" benefit from a visit.
E. limit the number of visitors to New York by discouraging those who are not qualified to enjoy it.

43.7 TONE

It is apparent from this passage that the author's feelings about New York as an attraction are
A. identified with native New Yorkers.
B. jaded.
C. moderately approving.
D. both approving and disapproving.
E. enthusiastically approving.

43.8 VOCABULARY

By "open sesame" the author means
A. a guidebook to the best places in New York.
B. a means of benefiting from the city's offerings.
C. a way to understand the peculiar language of the Big City.
D. a warm welcome.
E. a focus of interest.

Propaganda is the most terrible weapon so far developed. It is worse than poison gas. If the wind is in the right direction, gas may kill a few and injure others; but the possibilities of manipulating the public mind by withholding or discoloring the facts are appalling. One is so helpless in the face of it. No one can think intelligently without knowing the facts; and if the facts are controlled by **interested** men, the very idea of democracy is destroyed and becomes a farce.

─────────────────── Questions for Passage #44 ───────────────────

44.1
SUBJECT MATTER

The passage focuses on
A. the deadliness of propaganda.
B. the helplessness of people faced with propaganda.
C. how propaganda compares with poison gas as a weapon.
D. the defeating of democracy.
E. how propaganda alters the facts.

44.2
GENERALIZATION

The main thought of this passage is that
A. propaganda is worse than poison gas.
B. propaganda is the most terrible weapon yet developed.
C. propaganda seeks to control the facts we need.
D. propaganda destroys democracy.
E. we are helpless in the face of propaganda.

44.5
CONCLUSION

Democracy becomes farcial when facts are controlled because
A. people tend to laugh at a weak government which allows interested men to control facts.
B. people are not wise enough to penetrate propaganda.
C. a powerful few can control public opinion.
D. people are denied the vote.
E. people lack real information upon which to make decisions.

44.8
VOCABULARY

"Interested" men are men who
A. lie about facts.
B. look forward to learning the facts.
C. stand to gain if the public thinks in a certain way.
D. have been asked to control the facts.
E. stand to suffer by propaganda.

44.9
COMMUNICATION TECHNIQUE

The third sentence of the passage shows
A. why one is helpless in the face of propaganda.
B. how the public mind can be manipulated.
C. the analogy between wind and propaganda.
D. why propaganda is worse than poison gas.
E. none of the above.

For the globe as a whole, the ocean is the great regulator, the great stabilizer of temperatures. It has been described as a "savings bank for solar energy, receiving deposits in seasons of want." Without the ocean, our world would be visited by unthinkably harsh extremes of temperature. For the water that covers three-fourths of the earth's surface with an enveloping mantle is a substance of remarkable qualities. It is an excellent absorber and radiator of heat. Because of its enormous heat capacity, the ocean can absorb a great deal of heat from the sun without becoming what we would consider "hot," or it can lose much of its heat without becoming "cold."

Through the agency of ocean currents, heat and cold may be distributed over thousands of miles. It is possible to follow the course of a mass of warm water that originates in the tradewind belt of the Southern Hemisphere and remains recognizable for a year and a half, through a course of more than 7,000 miles. This redistributing function of the ocean tends to make up for the uneven heating of the globe by the sun. As it is, ocean currents carry hot equatorial water toward the poles and return cold water equator-ward by such surface drifts as the Labrador Current and Oyashio, and even more importantly, by deep currents. The redistribution of heat for the whole earth is accomplished about half by the ocean currents, and half by the winds.

At that thin interface between the ocean of water and the ocean of overlying air, lying as they do in direct contact over by far the greater part of the earth, there are continuous interactions of tremendous importance.

The atmosphere warms or cools the ocean. It receives vapors through evaporation, leaving most of the salts in the sea and so increasing the salinity of the water. With the changing weight of that whole mass of air that envelops the earth, the atmosphere brings variable pressure to bear on the surface of the sea, which is depressed under areas of high pressure and springs up in compensation under the atmospheric lows. With the moving force of the winds, the air grips the surface of the ocean and raises it into waves, drives the currents onward, lowers sea level on lee shores, and raises it on windward shores.

But even more does the ocean dominate the air. Its effect on the temperature and humidity of the atmosphere is far greater than the small transfer of heat from air to sea. It takes 3,000 times as much heat to warm a given volume of water 1° as to warm an equal volume of air by the same amount. The heat lost by a cubic meter of water on cooling 1°C would raise the temperature of 3,000 cubic meters of air by the same amount. Or to use another example, a layer of water a meter deep, on cooling .1° could warm a layer of air 33 meters thick by 10°. The temperature of the air is intimately related to atmospheric pressure. Where the air is cold, pressure tends to be high; warm air favors low pressures. The transfer of heat between ocean and air therefore alters the belts of high and low pressure; this profoundly affects the direction and strength of the winds and directs the storms on their paths.

There are six more or less permanent centers of high pressure over the oceans, three in each hemisphere. Not only do these areas play a controlling part in the climate of surrounding lands, but they affect the whole world because they are the birthplaces of most of the dominant winds of the globe. The trade winds originate in high-pressure belts of the Northern and

Southern hemispheres. Over all the vast extent of ocean across which they blow, these great winds retain their identity; it is only over the continents that they become interrupted, confused, and modified.

In other ocean areas there are belts of low pressure which develop, especially in winter, over waters that are then warmer than the surrounding lands. Traveling barometric depressions or cyclonic storms are attracted by these areas; they move rapidly across them or skirt around their edges. So winter storms take a path across the Icelandic "low" and over the Shetlands and Orkneys into the North Sea and the Norwegian Sea; other storms are directed by still other low pressure areas over the Skagerrak and the Baltic into the interior of Europe. Perhaps more than any other condition, the low-pressure area over the warm water south of Iceland dominates the winter climate of Europe.

And most of the rains that fall on sea and land alike were raised from the sea. They are carried as vapor in the winds, and then with change of temperature the rains fall. Most of the European rain comes from evaporation of Atlantic water. In the United States, vapor and warm air from the Gulf of Mexico and the tropical waters of the western Atlantic ride the winds up the wide valley of the Mississippi and provide rains for much of the eastern part of North America.

Whether any place will know the harsh extremes of a continental climate or the moderating effect of the sea depends less on its nearness to the ocean than on the pattern of currents and winds and the relief of the continents. The east coast of North America receives little benefit from the sea, because the prevailing winds are from the west. The Pacific coast, on the other hand, lies in the path of the westerly winds that have blown across thousands of miles of ocean. The moist breath of the Pacific brings climatic mildness and creates the dense rain forests of British Columbia, Washington, and Oregon; but its full influence is largely restricted to a narrow strip by the coast ranges that follow a course parallel to the sea. Europe, in contrast, is wide open to the sea, and "Atlantic weather" carries hundreds of miles into the interior.

─────────────── Questions for Passage #45 ───────────────

45.2
GENERALIZATION

The redistribution of heat for the whole earth is accomplished
A. primarily by the oceans.
B. primarily by the winds.
C. about half by the ocean currents and half by the winds.
D. by the equator.
E. by low pressure areas.

45.3 (a)
DETAIL

The oceans of the world have been compared to a great regulator because they

A. give off heat.   D. store and distribute heat.
B. absorb heat.   E. warm the atmosphere.
C. regulate the trade winds.

45.3 (b)
DETAIL

Warm water is carried by ocean currents from the
A. South Pole toward the equator.
B. equator toward the North Pole.
C. poles toward the equator.
D. North Pole toward the equator.
E. equator toward the poles.

Go on to next page. ➤

**45.3 (c)
DETAIL**

Ocean currents which run deep below the surface of the ocean
A. are cold currents running from the poles to the equator.
B. are warm currents running from the poles to the equator.
C. are not influenced by surface currents.
D. have a higher salt content than surface currents.
E. are not influenced by temperatures.

**45.3 (d)
DETAIL**

The transfer of heat between ocean and air
A. cools the ocean.
B. is minimal.
C. changes the direction of the ocean currents.
D. heats the air.
E. changes the belts of high and low pressure.

**45.6
APPLICATION**

Assume that just north of subtropical Los Angeles and a few miles in from the coast lie a range of mountains. Beyond these mountains is Ojai Valley. Based on the principles described in the passage you would expect to find Ojai Valley
A. and the seacoast having almost identical climates.
B. rainier than the seacoast.
C. cooler than the hotter seacoast.
D. hotter than the milder seacoast.
E. none of the above.

46

Animal populations are governed by food supplies, the number of animals of a particular type that are alive at a given time being just the number that can be supported with the food supply available at that time. Let the food supply increase, and the number of animals increases. Let the food supply decrease, and the number of animals decreases, starvation being the controlling factor.

— Questions for Passage #46 —

**46.1
SUBJECT MATTER**

This passage centers about
A. the relationship between the total number of animals and the number of animals of any one particular type.
B. why animal populations increase.
C. the relationship between animal population and available food.
D. why starvation is the controlling factor in the size of animal population.
E. why animal populations decrease.

**46.2
GENERALIZATION**

The main thought of this passage is that
A. increased food supply will result in more animals.
B. starvation limits the size of animal population.
C. decreased food supply will result in fewer animals.
D. the size of an animal population depends upon the food available.
E. animals who gather food can rule their fellows.

46.5
CONCLUSION

According to this passage, which of the following factors remains constant?

A. number of animals alive.
B. available food supply.
C. animals alive and available food supply.
D. number of types of animals alive.
E. amount of food needed by an animal for survival.

46.6
APPLICATION

Assume that a hamster needs 6 pellets per day to survive, and that a mink needs 12 pellets. If minks and hamsters alternate in eating, with a mink eating first, and there are 180 pellets for each day, how many hamsters could survive if we follow the formula implied in the passage?

A. 6
B. 8
C. 10
D. 15
E. 24

47

Man is called by nature to live in society; for he needs many things which are necessary to his life, and which by himself he cannot procure for himself. Whence it follows that man naturally becomes part of a group, to procure him the means of living well. He needs this assistance for two reasons. First, in order that he may obtain the elementary necessities of life; this he does in the domestic circle of which he is a part. Every man receives from his parents life and nourishment and education; and the reciprocal aid of the family members facilitates the mutual provision of the necessities of life. But there is a second reason why the individual is helped by the group of which he is a part, and in which alone he finds his adequate well-being. And this is, that he may not only live, but live the good life — which is enabled by the opportunities of social intercourse. Thus civil society aids the individual in obtaining the material necessities, by uniting in the same city a great number of crafts, which could not be so united in the same family. And civil society also assists him in the moral life.

———————————— Questions for Passage #47 ————————————

47.1
SUBJECT MATTER

The best title for this passage is:
A. How Man Lives the Moral Life.
B. How Man Lives the Good Life.
C. How Society Helps Man.
D. The Social Nature of Man.
E. How Man Obtains the Material Necessities of Life.

47.2
GENERALIZATION

Man becomes part of a group because he wishes to fulfill certain needs. One need *not* specifically mentioned by the passage is the need

A. for love and affection.
B. for a moral life.
C. for material necessities.
D. for education.
E. to live the good life.

47.3
DETAIL

The author mentions that cities contain a great number of crafts. These crafts enable the individual to

A. provide himself with social change.
B. increase the variety of his material necessities.
C. get a job.
D. live a more moral life because the crafts bring together many people with whom the individual must get along.
E. secure the elementary necessities of life.

Owing to the existence of three rivers, themselves the product of the more **remote** geographical conditions of relief and climate, China has produced a homogeneous people, whose essential unity has been strengthened by the existence on the west of a plateau of enormous breadth (Tibet). These two sets of features, the river system and the plateau, are the chief controls of Chinese history.

Other geographical conditions have had a like result; the position of China fronting the open ocean, on the road to nowhere by sea, and the absence of any Mediterranean Sea, are great, silent, negative controls, which have to an incalculable degree tended to confirm the Chinese in their habits as landsmen, and to prevent their becoming seamen. Nor were the Chinese forced to take to the sea, as were the Norsemen, by the poverty of a cold, sterile land. There was no effective pressure behind as was the case with the Saxon. China is vast enough to allow such pressures as did come from the plateau or Manchuria to dissipate themselves ere the seaboard was reached, and there was always the southern land where these pressures were less felt. No major road reached the sea, as was the case with the Phoenicians. The coast of China is a great round curve with no peninsulas to tempt men seawards, as was the case with the Greeks. China has never been a seapower, because nothing has ever induced her peoples to be otherwise than landsmen, and landsmen dependent on agriculture, with the same habits and ways of thinking drilled into them through forty centuries; so that even when tribes from the plateau have broken in and seized the reins of power, even when millions of inhabitants have been massacred, China has not broken up into numberless units, as did the Roman Empire. The homogeneity of her people, the result to a very large extent of geographical conditions, has always asserted itself.

───── Questions for Passage #48 ─────

48.3
DETAIL

In not being subject to the pressure of a hostile landscape, the Chinese were unlike the

A. Phoenicians.　　D. Tibetans.
B. Norsemen.　　E. Romans.
C. Greeks.

48.8
VOCABULARY

By "remote" conditions the author probably means conditions which are

A. present in the Chinese land mass.
B. distant in space.
C. distant in time.
D. political or cultural.
E. unknown.

48.9
COMMUNICATION
TECHNIQUE

The fact that China fronts the open sea on the road to nowhere is cited to show

A. why the Chinese were different from the Norsemen and the Saxons.
B. why the Chinese were dependent on agriculture.
C. why Chinese did not become seamen.
D. that Chinese were controlled in their character.
E. that negative controls are necessary if a people is to remain unified.

As early as the sixteenth centery it was noticed that a star in the constellation of the Whale appears and vanishes at irregular intervals. Its period — that is, the time between each reappearance — is roughly one year. Additional "variable" stars were found, and it was discovered that most of them do not vanish, like a light being switched on and off, but rather dim and brighten, often with a characteristic rhythm. With one class of variables it became evident that they are "waltzing" with a dark companion. When the latter comes between the earth and the visible star, the light of the latter is dimmed or eclipsed. However, another type dims slowly, then rises to maximum brightness rapidly, with accompanying changes in spectrum that show the star to be actually pulsing.

One of the most prominent of these stars appears in the constellation Cepheus; hence they are known as Cepheid variables (a category that in recent years has been further subdivided). The nearest and best known is Polaris, the North Star, whose pulse rate is 3.97 days. The periods of the various kinds of variable stars range from minutes to more than a year.

Toward the end of the nineteenth century the Harvard College Observatory began a systematic search for variables by comparing photographs taken of the same region of the heavens at different times. Various methods were used to speed up the process, such as laying a positive plate over a negative plate of the same star pattern, exposed at a different time, thus canceling out all stars whose brightness was unchanged. By 1910 some 4,000 variables were known, 3,000 of them discovered at Harvard. Data from the southern heavens was obtained at a field station operated by the university high among the Andes, at Arequipa, Peru. At the observatory in Massachusetts, Henrietta S. Leavitt studied the variables appearing in photographs of the two Clouds of Magellan, taken from Arequipa. These two clouds of stars are now classed as irregular galaxies and are our own galaxy's nearest neighbors in the cosmos.

Miss Leavitt and her co-workers listed 1,777 variables in the two clouds, and she picked for study those in the Small Magellanic Cloud for which reliable data on pulse rates and luminosity were available. In 1904 she published preliminary findings on seventeen of them; and eight years later, with firm data on eight more, she felt confident of her discovery.

"There is," she said, "a remarkable relation between the brightness of these variables and the lengths of their periods."

The slower the pulse rate of the star, the brighter its light, the rule being applicable both at maximum and minimum. She pointed out that the stars, clustered in a compact and extremely distant cloud, could all be considered the same distance away and therefore the differences in their brightness were intrinsic and not a result of differences in distance.

At first the discovery seemed of interest only in trying to explain why variable stars behave as they do. However, the Danish astronomer Ejnar Hertzsprung almost immediately saw the significance of these stars as a potential yardstick for the universe. Since the dimming of light by distance follows a well-established law, once the distance to one Cepheid variable was known, its intrinsic brightness could be calculated. Then, by simply timing the pulse rate of any other Cepheid, it would be possible to reckon its

Go on to next page. ➤

distance also. The trouble was that none were near enough so that their distance could be triangulated, even using the longest base line available to us: that joining opposite sides of the earth's orbit around the sun. However, a more crude method was available, namely that of analyzing rates of apparent movement against the stellar background. On the average, the faster a star changes position among the other stars, the nearer it is presumed to be. In this way Hertzsprung, in 1913, obtained rough distances for the thirteen nearby Cepheids on which he had adequate data. Shapley then attacked the same problem and the yardstick, though still imperfect, was forged.

The principle of the Cepheid yardstick can be envisioned in terms of a night sky filled with lighthouses flashing at what seem random rates. Some lights are brilliant; some so dim they can only be seen through binoculars; but their brightness cannot be used as a measure of distance, since it is known that some lighthouses contain lights of blinding brilliance, whereas others have bulbs of only a few watts. Then it is found that the rate at which each light flashes is an indication of its intrinsic brightness. All that then has to be done is to find the distance to one lighthouse in order to determine how far it is to all the others.

───────────────── Questions for Passage #49 ─────────────────

49.1
SUBJECT MATTER

The most suitable title for this passage would be:
A. The Nature of Variable Stars.
B. The Search for Variable Stars.
C. The Unknowable Universe.
D. The Methods of Astronomy.
E. Determining Stellar Distances.

49.2 (a)
GENERALIZATION

A major difference between the two types of variable stars mentioned is that
A. one is eclipsed by a non-luminous star while the other pulsates in brightness.
B. one type "waltzes" with another star while the second type remains stationary.
C. one type belongs to the Cepheid group while the second type is found primarily in the Magellan group.
D. the "waltzing" variety is still mostly uncharted.
E. relating to the degree of their luminosity.

49.2 (b)
GENERALIZATION

A variable star is, in general,
A. brighter than another variable of longer pulsation period.
B. brighter than another variable of shorter period of pulsation.
C. darker than its non-luminous twin.
D. nearer to earth at its maximum brightness.
E. a star of the third magnitude.

49.5
CONCLUSION

Once the relationship between pulse rate and brightness had been worked out, the astronomers needed to know
A. the distance of one of the Cepheid variables.
B. the way lighthouses work on earth.
C. the actual brightness of one variable.
D. how to find a base for triangulating a star.
E. the relationship between distance and brightness.

Any question whatever about the sentiment of the working or poorer class at any time in history is difficult to answer. Until recently, a serious portrait of the poor, even in literature, was unheard of. As in Shakespeare's plays, they were usually put in to inject a note of levity or buffoonery. Today, with all the presumed improvements in methods of social investigation and research, the workers somehow defy detection and examination. In public opinion polls they are usually underestimated; in political studies they vanish into apathy; in sociological studies they prefer silence or evasion, leaving the stage to others more practiced in reading and writing. Like the slaves of antiquity, workers stay in the shadow of the public realm.

For this reason I regard with suspicion the contention that the gospel of work absorbed the working class. Its aim was to do that, of course, and, since it was expounded by persons of influence and position, no doubt many on the lower rungs paid it lip service. We can assert with greater certainty that a pious attitude toward work existed among the proprietors and the clerical classes. In attenuated form it exists among such classes today. The worker probably never lost the idea of work as a means to a livelihood, though the work ethic may have infiltrated his class in the encouragement of regularity, honesty, application, and, certainly, respect for the clock. In 1848 when Charles A. Dana was in Paris as the *Tribune's* correspondent, the workers told him, "All we want is bread." He was a good reporter, fresh from another land, and although favoring the workers — "I had gone among the workers and ascertained the sentiments that animated them" — he had not gone overboard for them. Anyone who has punched a clock in a present-day factory can adduce current evidence to show that while there is more than bread on the workers' minds, there is little of the gospel of work.

In the factory, an underground life is lived under the noses of foremen, supervisors, and time-study men. They may smell it, but they find it hard to see or touch. The workers live in a world apart, on its negative side slow, restrictive, inimical to supervisors, management, and other outsiders; on its positive side inventive, ingenious, and loyal to co-workers. The experienced worker does everything possible, including purposely springing frames and burning up drills to put time-study men off their calculations and set a slower time estimate for the job. No mean dramatic ability comes to the fore in the effort: the worker jumps around the machine, steaming and sweating at every pore. Once management's man is out of range, the job goes back to the pace the workers themselves have decided to keep. They set a job at a certain pace, or fix an output quota, not only to keep from being speeded up but to avoid having their pay rates lowered. They often devise their own mechanical inventions and gimmicks which they apply to their machines once the cat is away. Anyone who tries to work faster than the informally set pace soon **finds himself in Coventry** — or even loses his job.

If the work ethic ever possessed such men, it has by now oozed away. No one maintains the this attitude characterizes every American worker: there are also the rate-busters. Great variations exist among workers, as any experienced foreman knows. Even their point of origin has importance — workers in a town full of Scotch-Irish descendants will work differently from those in a town with mixed nationalities. Workers newly arrived from the South or rural areas perform their job differently from those from other sections or the cities. The interesting thing at the moment is that to a surface observer these men, goldbrickers and rate-busters alike, might all seem to be hard at work, imbued with the zeal of missionary monks or Protestant reformers. Underneath the surface, there may be nothing of the sort. They may be plotting — all in a spirit of fun and fellowship — where to hide one another's wrenches or when to cut off the gas to the welder's line.

—————————————————— Questions for Passage #50 ——————————————————

50.1
SUBJECT MATTER

A good title for this passage would be:
A. The Inarticulate Working Class.
B. Workers and History.
C. Workers Do Not Live by Bread Alone.
D. The Attitude of the Working Class Towards Work.
E. The Secret Life of the Working Class.

50.5
CONCLUSION

We may conclude from this passage that workers work chiefly to
A. play tricks on each other.
B. participate in social relationships within the factory.
C. earn a livelihood.
D. gain a feeling of achievement.
E. outwit their enemies, the upper class.

50.7
TONE

The author expresses a kind of admiration of working people when he says
A. in political studies workers vanish into oblivion.
B. regularity , honesty, application, and a respect for the clock have infiltrated the working class.
C. variations exist among workers of different origins.
D. the experienced worker does everything possible to put time-study men off . . . and no mean dramatic ability comes to the fore.
E. to a surface observer these men . . . seem . . . imbued with the zeal of missionary monks.

50.8
VOCABULARY

The last sentence in the third paragraph states, "Anyone who tries to work faster than the informally set pace soon finds himself in Coventry — or even loses his job." A worker who "finds himself in Coventry" is one who
A. feels the weight of unpopularity among his co-workers.
B. wears himself out.
C. is strongly reprimanded by his foreman.
D. is in favor with management.
E. is forced to move to a new factory.

If the earth were a smooth sphere like a billiard ball without mountains or vegetation upon it, and if it were devoid of oceans and did not spin on its axis each twenty-four hours, and if in some manner the sun succeeded in warming all parts of the Equator, the general circulation of the atmosphere would be a fairly simple problem. The air along the Equator would rise and move toward the North Pole in the Northern Hemisphere and toward the South Pole in the Southern. Cooler air in the upper latitudes would flow along the surface toward the Equator in both hemispheres. Thus all surface winds would blow away from the poles and all upper winds would blow toward them.

Unfortunately for anyone who assays the task of understanding the winds, it is far from anything quite so simple as this. There are plenty of complications to befuddle even the clearest head. For the difference in temperature of land and water has its influence on the winds, as well as the temperature between day and night. The winds, too, are affected by heat rising from the various continents, or by the lack of heat in others, or by the fact that the sun's rays at different seasons strike the various parts of our earth at different angles. Again, the mountains affect the winds and the presence of great forests that check their flow or create downward drafts, while deserts affect the winds with currents sweeping upward from their burning sands. There is the effect of moisture that the winds gather as they pass over the seven seas, and then, besides all these and more, there is the devious influence which the rotation of the earth has upon all the winds.

This last aspect of the problem is the most disconcerting one of all, for the effect of the earth's rotation is both real and only apparent, involving a student in the thorny problem of relativity. Though to us the great Trade Winds, for example, move **obliquely** across the face of the earth, from the moon's eye view they move almost directly north and south.

It is a simple enough matter to demonstrate this graphically. Take an orange, and while you revolve it from left to right as the earth moves, draw upon its surface with a ballpoint pen (it will leave a mark) a perpendicular line following the direction of the axis from what represents the North Pole to the Equator. You will observe that the line you have drawn is curved and that it veers to the right, or, in terms of the compass, toward the southwest. Now draw a perpendicular line from the South Pole as you revolve the orange. This line will veer toward the left.

When this deflection is applied to winds, it is called the Coriolis Force. Some say it is improperly named, being an effect rather than a force; for the direction mainly depends on one's point of view — whether one is on the earth or somewhere out in space. But in order to avoid involving the reader at this moment in that bewildering problem, we can leave it for the nonce, or for good, and merely point out that this veering, actual or apparent, has its effect on the direction of the winds. Rotation of the earth makes the Trade Winds in the Northern Hemisphere blow toward the southwest, and it also causes for less obvious reasons a hurricane or any wind circulating around a low pressure area to move counterclockwise north of the Equator and clockwise south of it.

Go on to next page. ➤

51.1
SUBJECT MATTER

A good title for this selection would be:
A. Mountains, Deserts, Forests, and Winds.
B. The Movement of Winds.
C. The Coriolis Force.
D. Science Can Be Simple.
E. Winds of the World.

51.2
GENERALIZATION

The Coriolis Force is
A. the cause of air currents rising at the equator.
B. the deflection of winds by mountains and deserts.
C. the effect of the earth's rotation upon the winds.
D. the cause of air currents settling at the poles.
E. not a true influence on the earth's winds.

51.3
DETAIL

If the earth were stationary, the prevailing direction of the earth's surface winds would be
A. sourth to north.
B. north to south.
C. from the equator to the poles.
D. from the poles to the equator.
E. counterclockwise.

51.8
VOCABULARY

The author states that the Trade Winds move obliquely across the face of the earth. By "obliquely" he means that the winds move
A. north to south.
B. south to north.
C. east to west.
D. north to west.
E. west to east.

52

The single business of Henry Thoreau, during forty-odd years of eager activity, was to discover an economy calculated to provide a satisfying life. His one concern, that give to his ramblings in Concord fields a value of high adventure, was to explore the true meaning of wealth. As he understood the problem of economics, there were three possible solutions open to him: to exploit himself, to exploit his fellows, or to reduce the problem to its lowest denominator. The first was quite impossible — to imprison oneself in a treadmill when the morning called to great adventure. To exploit one's fellows seemed to Thoreau's sensitive social conscience an even greater infidelity. Freedom with abstinence seemed to him better than serfdom with material well-being, and he was content to move to Walden Pond and to set about the high business of living, "to front only the essential facts of life and to see what it had to teach." He did not advocate that other men should build cabins and live isolated. He had no wish to dogmatize concerning the best mode of living — each must settle that for himself. But that a satisfying life should be lived, he was vitally concerned. The story of his emancipation from the lower economics is the one romance of his life, and *Walden* is his great book. It is a book in praise of life rather than of Nature, a record of calculating economics that studied saving in order to spend more largely. But it is a book of social criticism as well, in spite of its explicit denial of such a purpose. In considering the true nature of economy he concluded, with Ruskin, that the cost of a thing is the amount of life which is required in exchange for it, immediately or in the long run. In *Walden* Thoreau elaborated the text: "The only wealth is life."

52.1
SUBJECT MATTER

The best title for this passage would be:
A. Thoreau's Theory of the Good Life.
B. Thoreau's Ethics.
C. *Walden*, Thoreau's Greatest Work.
D. How Thoreau Saved Money.
E. Life at Walden Pond.

52.2 (a)
GENERALIZATION

Thoreau's primary aim in life was to
A. do as little work as possible.
B. work out the best adjustment to economic facts.
C. convert others to his way of life.
D. discover what nature could tell us about how to live.
E. emancipate himself from the demands of society.

52.2 (b)
GENERALIZATION

Thoreau's solution to the problem of living was to
A. study Nature.   D. make other men work for him.
B. work in a mill.   E. write for a living.
C. live in a simple way.

52.3
DETAIL

According to Thoreau, the wealth of an individual is measured by
A. the money he makes.   D. the books he creates.
B. the amount he saves.   E. his social standing.
C. the experience he gains.

52.5
CONCLUSION

Thoreau's attitude toward society can best be characterized as one of
A. hatred.   D. acceptance.
B. avoidance.   E. individualism.
C. didacticism.

53

Elizabeth Jane's position was indeed to a marked degree one that, in the common phrase, afforded much to be thankful for. That she was not demonstratively thankful was no fault of hers. Her experience had been of a kind to teach her, rightly or wrongly, that the doubtful honor of a brief transit through a sorry world hardly called for **effusiveness**, even when the path was suddenly irradiated at some halfway point by daybeams rich as hers. But her strong sense that neither she nor any human being deserved less than was given did not blind her to the fact that there were others receiving less who had deserved much more. And in being forced to class herself among the fortunate she did not cease to wonder at the persistence of the unforeseen, when the one to whom such unbroken tranquility had been accorded in the adult stage was she whose youth had seemed to teach that happiness was but the occasional episode in a general drama of pain.

―――――――――――――――― Questions for Passage #53 ――――――――――

53.2
GENERALIZATION

The writer feels that
A. life is pleasant for most people.
B. life is a privilege for which we should be grateful.
C. most of those who get little from this world deserve no more than they get.
D. Elizabeth Jane should have had a feeling of guilt for having been more fortunate than others.
E. life is generally painful.

Go on to next page. ➤

Elizabeth Jane's adult life can be classified as

A. tranquil.   D. painful.
B. extremely happy. E. lonely.
C. unhappy.

The word "effusiveness" means

A. excessive emotion. D. complaining.
B. display of moroseness. E. blame.
C. questioning.

54

Regardless of the source or kind of light, the ability of light to form an image is dependent upon just one thing — a small hole or a *lens* to bring the rays to a focus. The principle of image formation was discovered in early Greek times. Later it was realized that the eye itself has a lens and that an image is, in fact, formed on the *retina*, the rear inside surface of the eyeball. Some man inside a cave or a darkened room noticed that light entering through a small hole in the wall or in the hide covering of the door formed an image on the far wall. It was observed that if you enlarged the hole, the image blurred and disappeared. On the other hand, the smaller the hole, the sharper the image — down to a certain diameter after which making the hole smaller makes the image worse again.

The function of a pinhole is to screen out all light rays except those coming in a perfectly straight line from the object, thus improving the sharpness of the image. After passing through a point (the pinhole) the rays again spread out a little bit, and the size of the image formed will depend upon how far back the wall, screen, or film is from the pinhole. You can try this yourself in a completely darkened room with a pinhole in a window shade. Simply by moving a piece of white cardboard first near the hole, and gradually backward, you can observe the image grow in size and also get dimmer as it becomes bigger. It takes more light to make a bright, large image than a small image of the same brightness.

The full exploitation of this phenomenon had to wait for the development of the lens, which gathered in a much larger number of light rays and still brought them to form an image, just as the pinhole did, but with a difference: in a pinhole camera, the light rays form an image that is equally sharp regardless of the distance to the film. When a lens is used, there may be a choice of planes of focus determined by adjusting the lens-to-film distance. Each plane is located some distance behind and relatively parallel to the lens.

* * * * * * * * * *

Actual blown glass was developed early in Egyptian times, and the first lens may have been the bottom of a wine bottle. However, the first deliberate grinding of lenses did not take place until the thirteenth century, and the art did not become established until the sixteenth century. A book on the grinding and polishing of lenses was issued by B. Battista della Porta in 1589, but it was not until 1611 that Kepler compared a lens of glass to the lens in the eye and showed that rays from each point of an object were brought to a focus at each corresponding point of an image on the retina.

Then, in 1619, Scheiner demonstrated the actual formation of an inverted image on the retina by taking an eye from a cadaver, cutting a window in the side of the eyeball, and observing the image directly.

Among the first uses of the lens, in addition to its use as a magnifier and burning glass, may have been as a substitute for the original pinhole in big room-size cameras — called camera obscuras. The name means "dark chamber" and originally the viewers entered the room to see the image formed on the back wall. The modern camera, although still a "chamber," is greatly reduced in size. With the addition of a mirror to invert the image, the camera obscura was used by artists to draw pictures from nature.

────────────────── Questions for Passage #54 ──────────────────

54.1
SUBJECT MATTER

A good title for this selection would be:
A. Modern Lenses.
B. The Modern Camera.
C. Lenses and Image Formation.
D. Developments in Photography.
E. The Human Eye.

54.2
GENERALIZATION

A camera lens is preferable to a pinhole because it can
A. offer a choice of planes of focus.
B. gather more light rays.
C. invert the light rays so that they may register on the film.
D. gather more light rays and bring them to a focus at a given plane.
E. control the size of the image formed on the film.

54.3
DETAIL

The principle of inverted image formation
A. was discovered by Battista della Porta in 1589.
B. was not understood until the first lens had been manufactured.
C. was thoroughly understood by cavemen.
D. is independent of the presence or absence of a lens or pinhole.
E. was demonstrated by a human eye.

54.5
CONCLUSION

The author compares the pinhole to a lens in order to show
A. the development of the lens.
B. that both operate on the same principle.
C. how the early camera operated.
D. how primitive scientific thinking was, prior to the 16th century.
E. how the *camera obscuras* worked.

55

"Everyone knows that in the stilly night we hear things unnoticed in the noise of day. The gentle ticking of the clock, the air circulating through the chimney, the cracking of the chairs in the room, and a thousand other slight noises, impress themselves upon our ear. It is equally well known that in the confused hubbub of the streets, or the clamor of a railway, we may lose not only what our neighbor says to us, but even not hear the sound of our own voice. The stars which are brightest at night are invisible by day; and although we see the moon then, she is far paler than at night. Everyone who has had to deal with weights knows that if to a pound in the hand a second pound is added, the difference is immediately felt; whilst if it be added to a hundredweight, we are not aware of the difference at all . . . .

Go on to next page. ➤

"The sound of the clock, the light of the stars, the pressure of the pound, these are all *stimuli* to our senses, and stimuli whose outward amount remains the same. What then do these experiences teach? Evidently nothing but this, that one and the same stimulus, according to circumstances under which it operates, will be felt either more or less intensely, or not felt at all. Of what sort now is the alteration in the circumstances upon which this alteration in the feeling may depend? On considering the matter closely, we see that it is everywhere of one and the same kind. The tick of the clock is a feeble stimulus for our auditory nerve, which we hear plainly when it is one, but not when it is added to the strong stimulus of the carriage-wheels and other noises of the day. The light of the stars is a stimulus to the eye. But if the stimulation which this light exerts be added to the strong stimulus of daylight, we feel nothing of it, although we feel it distinctly when it unites itself with the feebler stimulation of the twilight. The pound-weight is a stimulus to our skin, which we feel when it joins itself to a preceding stimulus of equal strength, but which vanishes when it is combined with a stimulus a thousand times greater in amount.

"We may therefore lay it down as a general rule that a stimulus, in order to be felt, may be so much the smaller if the already pre-existing stimulation of the organ is small, but must be so much the larger, the greater the pre-existing stimulation is . . . The simplest relation would obviously be that the sensation should increase in identically the same ratio as the stimulus . . . . But if this simplest of all relations prevailed . . . the light of the stars, *e.g.*, ought to make as great an addition to the daylight as it does to the darkness of the nocturnal sky, and this we know to be not the case . . . So it is clear that the strength of the sensations does not increase in proportion to the amount of the stimuli, but more slowly. And now comes the question, in what proportion does the increase of the sensation grow less as the increase of the stimulus grows greater? To answer this question, everyday experiences do not suffice. We need exact measurements, both of the amounts of the various stimuli, and of the intensity of the sensations themselves.

"How to execute these measurements, however, is something which daily experience suggests. To measure the strength of sensations is, as we saw, impossible; we can only measure the difference of sensations. Experience showed us that very unequal differences of sensation might come from equal differences of outward stimulus.

"But all these experiences expressed themselves in one kind of fact, that the same difference of stimulus could in one case be felt, and in another case not felt at all — a pound felt if added to another pound, but not if added to a hundredweight . . . We can quickest reach a result with our observations if we start with an arbitrary strength of stimulus, notice what sensation it gives us, and then *see how much we can increase the stimulus without making the sensation seem to change*. If we carry out such observations with stimuli of varying absolute amounts, we shall be forced to choose in an equally varying way the amounts of addition to the stimulus which are capable of giving us a just barely perceptible feeling of *more*. A light to be just perceptible in the twilight need not be near as bright as the starlight; it must be far brighter to be just perceived during the day. If now we institute such observations for all possible strengths of the various stimuli, and note for each strength the amount of addition of the latter required to produce a barely perceptible alteration of sensation, we shall have a series of figures in which is immediately expressed the law according to which the sensation alters when the stimulation is increased. . . ."

————————————— Questions for Passage #55 —————————————

55.1
SUBJECT MATTER

This passage is mainly about
A. variations in human sensations.
B. the nature of sensation.
C. the relationship between stimuli and sensations.
D. the indeterminate effects of stimuli.
E. the measurement of stimuli.

55.2 (a)
GENERALIZATION

The main idea of the passage is that
A. the effects of stimuli are too complex to be understood by man.
B. sensation increases in the same ratio as the stimulus increases.
C. we can determine the effects of stimuli through appropriate research.
D. the effect of a stimulus depends on the intensity of the pre-existing stimulus.
E. the effect of a given stimulus is not in direct proportion to its intensity.

55.2 (b)
GENERALIZATION

Another GENERALIZATION of the passage is that, as the strength of a given stimulus increases, the resulting change in sensation
A. increases proportionately.
B. increases in the same amount as the increase in the stimulus.
C. can be accurately measured.
D. can be determined by everyday common sense.
E. varies according to a hypothetical formula.

55.3
DETAIL

If a pre-existing sensation is intense because of a large pre-existing stimulus, a tiny additional stimulus of the same nature would tend to produce
A. no perceptible sensation.
B. a barely perceptible sensation.
C. a small additional sensation.
D. a large additional sensation.
E. a loss of some of the pre-existing sensation.

55.5
CONCLUSION

The author proposes to observe the effect on sensation of increasing stimuli by a series of arbitrary amounts. He expects from these observations to find the law by which sensation alters as stimulation is increased. His basic premise upon which the observations will be made is that
A. all possible strengths of a stimulus can be determined.
B. we can measure difference in, but not amount of, sensation.
C. the same stimulus may produce varying sensations.
D. daily experience gives the clue to executing the observations.
E. stated by none of the above.

Without attempting a rigorous definition, we can define music generally as a pleasing combination of sounds. Oddly enough, physicists tell us that notes which make harmonious combinations have frequencies (number of vibrations per second) that can be expressed *in the ratio of small whole numbers.* For example, the *octave* consists of two tones whose frequencies have the ratio 2:1. Another harmonious combination is the *fifth*, whose frequency ration is 3:2. One of the most pleasing combinations of all is the *major chord* consisting of three tones having a frequency ratio of 4:5:6. An example may serve to show how this works. The C major chord is made up of the notes C, E, and G. The frequencies of these notes (in the *physical scale* used by physicists) are 256, 320, and 384 vibrations per second, respectively. If each of these frequencies is divided by 64, the resulting numbers are 4, 5, and 6. These notes, therefore, are in the ratio of 4:5:6. In a similar manner, the *minor chords* are made up of notes in the ratio of 10:12:15. Now let's investigate a discordant combination of notes. If F and E are played together too often, most musicians rapidly lose their audience. These notes are in the ratio 853:1600. The fact that F and E are not in the ratio of small whole numbers seems to make them sound discordant to the human ear.

─────── Questions for Passage #56 ───────

56.1
SUBJECT MATTER

The best title for this passage would be:
A. Music as Mathematics.
B. The Physics of Music.
C. Pleasing Chords and Octaves.
D. Dissonances in Music.
E. Why Some Musicians Lose Their Audiences.

56.5
CONCLUSION

A note with a frequency of 512 vibrations per second would be
A. pleasing.
B. unpleasing.
C. indeterminate as to its quality.
D. hard to hear because of the high frequency.
E. a minor chord.

56.6
APPLICATION

A harmonious combination of two notes would most like fall into a frequency ratio of
A. 64:400.
B. 1:20.
C. 16:59.
D. 4:5.
E. none of the above.

56.7
TONE

The writer feels that the mathematical explanation of harmony is
A. expected.
B. fascinating.
C. easily understood.
D. incorrect.
E. curious.

Psychiatric tests show that a well-balanced person gets much angrier when provoked than an abnormal person does. At the New York State Psychiatric Institute, Dr. James Page and Professor of Psychology Carney Landis of Columbia University studied the reaction of 200 normals and 210 abnormals. They tested their reactions to maddening situations of every type and variety, such as: being laughed at and ridiculed, being repeatedly disconnected on the telephone, accidentally hitting their thumb with a hammer, being worked on by a backseat driver, being told to "shut up" and mind their own business, discovering someone cheating in a friendly card game, etc. In almost every instance the anger reaction of the normal group was much more intense than that of the abnormal one.

"This," they reported, "is in accord with other psychiatric findings. For one of the outstanding symptoms of mental unbalance is an emotional **apathy**." So if you blow your top when you bang you shin against a piece of furniture, or when your sweetheart goes out with another guy — don't worry about it. It's just a sign that you're normal.

─────────── Questions for Passage #57 ───────────

57.1
SUBJECT MATTER

This passage deals mainly with the
A. similarity to previous psychiatric studies of New York State Psychological Institute's findings concerning anger reactions.
B. absence of apathy in normals.
C. nature of incidents tending to provoke anger in normals versus abnormals.
D. level of intensity in anger reactions registered by normals versus abnormals.
E. frequency of anger reactions registered by normals versus abnormals.

57.2
GENERALIZATION

The main idea of this passage is that
A. anger is a unviersal phenomenon among humans.
B. psychiatric tests proved that a person who gets angry is well-balanced.
C. normal persons are apt to get angry much more easily than abnormal persons.
D. normal persons react more intensely to anger-provoking situations than do abnormal individuals.
E. none of the individuals tested was able to see that the anger-provoking actions of the experimenters were "rigged."

57.4
SIGNIFICANCE

The author recommends that, if you tend to become angry, you should
A. treat it as a normal reaction.
B. not worry about what has made you angry.
C. try to control your anger.
D. become concerned.
E. do none of the above.

57.8
VOCABULARY

The word "apathy" means
A. need for affection.   D. lack of feeling.
B. confusion.   E. anger.
C. undue sensitivity.

57.9
COMMUNICATION TECHNIQUE

The last two sentences of the passages contain
A. the main idea.
B. an important DETAIL supporting the GENERALIZATION.
C. an unrelated comment about the SUBJECT MATTER.
D. an opinion of Drs. Page and Landis.
E. a suggestion from the author about what you should do about the GENERALIZATION.

By using power-driven machines in factories and by developing efficient mass production methods, Americans have greatly increased the ability of the individual worker to produce goods. Because the production of each worker has increased from year to year, Americans have been able to buy and use an increasing number of things to make their lives more pleasant and comfortable than those of their forefathers. It is hard to believe that automobiles, radios, motion pictures, frozen foods, electric refrigerators, to mention only a few items, have come into common use within the last thirty years.

───────────── Questions for Passage #58 ─────────────

**58.1
SUBJECT MATTER**

The subject matter of this passage is
A. the benefit of increased productivity.
B. more comfort for modern Americans.
C. mass production methods.
D. the rising productivity of the American worker.
E. the results of using power-driven machines.

**58.2
GENERALIZATION**

Which of the following sentences most closely summarizes the main idea of the passage?
A. By using power-driven machines and by developing efficient mass-production methods, Americans have greatly increased the ability of the individual worker to produce goods.
B. Because the production of each worker has increased from year to year, Americans have been able to buy and use an increasing number of things to make their lives more pleasant.
C. It is hard to believe that automobiles, radios, motion pictures, frozen foods, to mention only a few items, have come into use within the last thirty years.
D. Efficient production methods have increased the wages of the American worker.
E. Americans of today buy more luxuries than their forefathers.

**58.3
DETAIL**

The author states that the average American's life is more pleasant and comfortable than that of his forefathers. By "more pleasant and comfortable" the author means that the average American
A. has more leisure time than his forefathers.
B. does not work as hard as his forefathers because he uses machines.
C. finds life easier now than it was during the time of his forefathers.
D. has more useful commodities.
E. is affected by none of the above.

**58.9
COMMUNICATION
TECHNIQUE**

The author mentions "automobiles, radios, motion pictures," etc., to show
A. that these items are popular with most people.
B. how hard it is to believe the reality of modern inventions.
C. how large is the list of conveniences which have been invented in the last thirty years.
D. some of the benefits of increased productivity.
E. none of the above.

The development of the English language falls into three reasonably distinct periods: Old English, from about A.D. 450, when the first Germanic tribes began to settle in England, until about 1100; Middle English, from about 1100 to about 1475; and Modern English, from about 1475 to the present. Of course the breaks were not as sudden and definite as these arbitrary dates indicate. There has never been a year when the language was not changing, or a time when it was spoken with anything like complete uniformity. Nevertheless, the characteristics of the three periods are so different that a person who knows both Old and Modern English well will find a good deal of difficulty in reading some of the Middle English writings without additional training.

———————————————— Questions for Passage #59 ————————————————

59.2
GENERALIZATION

The main idea of the passage is that

A. the development of the English language falls into three reasonably distinct periods.

B. the development of Middle English took place from 1100 - 1475.

C. it is difficult to distinguish different developmental stages of the English language.

D. English is essentially a Germanic language.

E. a speaker of Modern English would need training to read Middle English.

59.3
DETAIL

The development of Middle English took place during the period

A. 450 to 1100.

B. from the end of Old English to about 1475.

C. 1475 to the present.

D. 450 to the beginning of Modern English.

E. 1100 to the present.

59.5
CONCLUSION

In discussing the stages in the development of English, the author feels that

A. his scholarship has enabled him to mark their beginnings and endings precisely.

B. once the language shifted, it remained with little change until the time for the next major change.

C. during the years 1100 to 1475 many Englishmen probably needed additional training to make the transfer to the more fashionable tongue of their day.

D. the three major stages are reasonably separate and distinct although not completely uniform.

E. none of these statements is true.

60

The whole atmosphere of the world in which we live is tinged by science, as is shown most immediately and strikingly by our modern conveniences and material resources. A little deeper thinking shows that the influence of science goes much farther and colors the entire mental outlook of modern civilized man on the world about him. Perhaps one of the most telling evidences of this is his growing freedom from superstition. Freedom from superstition is the result of the conviction that the world is not governed by **caprice**, but that it is a world of order and can be understood by man if he will only try hard enough and be clever enough. This conviction that the world is understandable is, doubtless, the most important single gift of science to civilization. The wide-spread acceptance of this view can be dated to the discovery by Newton of the universal sway of the law of gravitation; and for this reason Newton may be justly regarded as the most important single contributor to modern life.

―――――――――――――― Questions for Passage #60 ――――――――――――――

60.1
SUBJECT MATTER

The title below that best expresses the SUBJECT MATTER of this passage is:

A. Science and Modern Conveniences.
B. Science and Civilization.
C. Important Scientific Principles.
D. Science and the World of Moral Order.
E. Discovery of Scientific Laws.

60.3
DETAIL

The greatest benefit of science has been

A. the encouragement of deep thinking.
B. the work of reconstruction.
C. the development of material resources.
D. an understanding that the world has order.
E. the rapid growth of everyday conveniences.

60.5
CONCLUSION

The passage implies that, prior to Newton,

A. men felt nature to be essentially inscrutable.
B. men were unable to cope with the chance factors in nature.
C. men understood nature but did not apply their knowledge.
D. the humanities were of little value.
E. men were interested in science chiefly for its practical contributions to their welfare.

60.7
TONE

We may reasonably conclude that the author of this passage may best be described as inclined to be

A. intuitive in his approaches to the major problems he is faced with.
B. rational in his approaches to problems.
C. rational in his approaches to problems and decisive in his conclusions.
D. sweeping in his generalizations and insufficiently reflective.
E. different from any of the above.

60.8
VOCABULARY

"Caprice" as used in the passage means

A. logic.   D. chance.
B. luck.   E. indolence.
C. power.

61

In a very real sense, then, people who have read good literature have lived more than people who cannot or will not read. To have read *Gulliver's Travels* is to have had the experience with Jonathan Swift, of turning sick at the stomach at the conduct of the human race; to read *Huckleberry Finn* is to feel what it is like to drift down the Mississippi River on a raft; to have read Byron is to have suffered with him his rebellions and neuroses and to have enjoyed with him his nose-thumbing at society; to have read *Native Son* is to know how it feels to be frustrated in the particular way in which Negroes in Chicago are frustrated. This is the great task that effective communication performs: it enables us to feel how others felt about life, even if they lived thousands of miles away and centuries ago. It is not true that "we have only one life to live"; if we can read, we can live as many more lives and as many kinds of lives as we wish.

—————————————— Questions for Passage #61 ——————————————

61.2 GENERALIZATION

The main thought of this passage is that

A. *Gulliver's Travels, Huckleberry Finn, Native Son,* and the work of Byron are examples of effective communication.

B. good literature helps us to have more experiences than we would if we did not read.

C. if we learn how to read effectively, we can increase the range of our experience.

D. people who read live more intensely than people who don't read.

E. effective communication helps us to know the feelings of people who are widely separated from us in space and time.

61.4 SIGNIFICANCE

The author is probably most interested in having the reader

A. be selective in his reading.

B. try to live more intensely.

C. learn about frustrated, disgusted, or rebellious people.

D. read more good literature.

E. read more, no matter what he reads.

61.5 CONCLUSION

The author of this passage assumes that people

A. enjoy suffering.

B. are interested in historical facts.

C. have read *Gulliver's Travels, Huckleberry Finn,* and *Native Son.*

D. can read effectively.

E. want to increase the range of their experience.

61.6 APPLICATION

According to the passage, which of the following would be *least* likely to fulfill the task of good literature?

A. a newspaper feature article about a fire

B. a science fiction novel

C. an account of the ascent of Mt. Everest

D. an operator's manual for a new car

E. a letter written by a child to his parents during his first week at summer camp

61.9 COMMUNICATION TECHNIQUE

The author refers to Jonathan Swift's "turning sick at the stomach at the conduct of the human race" to

A. interest the reader in reading *Gulliver's Travels.*

B. explain how Jonathan Swift felt about the human race.

C. express her own feelings about the human race.

D. show how we can identify with others' experiences through reading.

E. support none of the above.

In many cities persons of exceptional energy, taking advantage of some social conflict or class grievance, secured a more or less irregular power in the state. This combination of personality and opportunity has occurred in the United States of America, for example, where men exercising various kinds of informal power are called "bosses." In Greece they were called "tyrants." But the tyrant was rather more than a boss; he was recognized as a monarch, and claimed the authority of monarch. The modern boss, on the other hand, shelters behind legal forms which he has "got hold of" and uses for his own ends. Tyrants were distinguished from kings, who claimed some sort of right, some family priority, for example, to rule. They were supported, perhaps, by the poorer class with a grievance; Peisistratus, for example, who was tyrant of Athens, with two intervals of exile, between 560 and 527 B.C., was supported by the poverty-stricken Athenian hillmen. Sometimes, as in Greek Sicily, the tyrant stood for the rich against the poor. When, later on, the Persians began to subjugate the Greek cities of Asia Minor, they set up pro-Persian tyrants.

_____ Questions for Passage #62 _____

**62.1
SUBJECT MATTER**

This passage is mainly about
A. a comparison of Greek tyrants and modern bosses.
B. the modern "boss."
C. persons of exceptional energy who seized power.
D. the Greek "tyrant."
E. none of the above.

**62.3 (a)
DETAIL**

It could *not* be said of a Greek tyrant that he
A. was different from a modern boss because he ruled openly.
B. might be a person of exceptional energy.
C. ruled by inheritance.
D. claimed the authority of a monarch.
E. usually was supported by some particular class.

**62.3 (b)
DETAIL**

Peisistratus most probably ruled Athens
A. more than 33 years.
B. twice between 560 and 527 B.C.
C. three times after 527 B.C.
D. less than 33 years.
E. in a time interval not necessarily described by any of the above.

**62.5
CONCLUSION**

We may conclude that the tyrant's most important source of power was
A. the illegality of his position.
B. his own exceptional energy.
C. his forebears.
D. his position as monarch.
E. some segment of society whose cause he espoused.

**62.6
APPLICATION**

The two factors mentioned by the passage as making for the rise of tyrants were most probably not present in the case of
A. Franklin Roosevelt.   D. Calvin Coolidge.
B. Napoleon.   E. Winston Churchill.
C. Hitler.

How long, some reader will ask, has **the world** endured? That is a question which has attracted much attention in the last few years. Gradually the earlier estimates, which varied very widely, have been brought towards agreement. Astronomers and mathematicians who base their computations on the rate of cooling of celestial bodies and on various processes of diffusion and atomic change, give us 2,000 million years as the age of the earth as a body separate from the sun, and about 300 million years as the length of time since life appeared upon it in any abundance. The age of the sun as a star is now supposed to be somewhere in the nature of five million million years. The earth, says Sir James Jeans in his *Universe Around Us*, will in all probability go on for another million million years and then its equatorial temperature may be sinking to Arctic conditions. Since man has existed as a self-conscious social creature for only 30,000 years or less, this gives him illimitable opportunity for the attainment of knowledge and power. Long before he reaches that limit, he may make himself master of time and space.

—————————————————— Questions for Passage #63 ——————————————————

63.3
DETAIL

The period of time from the moment when the earth separated from the sun, until the time when life-sustaining conditions will no longer obtain is closest to

A. 2,000,000,000 years.
B. 102,000,000,000 years.
C. 400,000,000 years.
D. 5,000,000,000,000 years.
E. none of the above.

63.5
CONCLUSION

The author appears to feel that man will

A. ultimately have to adapt to arctic conditions.
B. become more self-conscious.
C. ultimately die out.
D. continue forever.
E. do none of the above.

63.8
VOCABULARY

By "the world" the author means

A. the solar system.
B. the earth.
C. the universe.
D. life as we know it.
E. the sun.

63.9
COMMUNICATION
TECHNIQUE

Part of the development of this passage consists of a question and an answer. Bearing this in mind, sentence 6 (containing the reference to Sir James Jeans) could best be considered as

A. part of the answer to the question.
B. a conclusion arrived at on the basis of the answer.
C. a statement of fact supporting the answer.
D. a supporting detail for a conclusion only indirectly related to the answer.
E. none of the above.

It is worth special comment that, while it is probably widely recognized that people who talk very little are likely to be not altogether well adjusted, it is not so generally understood that glibness is quite as significant in this respect. In fact, it seems to be commonly accepted that sustained and flowing speech is a mark of capability and intelligence. The very fact that in our culture a high value is placed on the "gift of gab" accounts, in no small part, for the nervous striving for volubility which some persons exhibit. It accounts also for the tendency of other individuals to lose confidence in their ability to speak acceptably and so to become relatively quiet. In our schools and universities speech is usually taught from the point of view that the ability to speak anywhere on any subject for any required length of time is very desirable. And yet every teacher doubtless has encountered many students whose verbal facility is found, on close examination, to represent a pathological or nearly pathological state. Educators might will give very serious consideration to this problem.

─────── Questions for Passage #64 ───────

64.2
GENERALIZATION

The main idea of this passage is that glibness in an individual is
A. always the result of praise for volubility.
B. not quite so significant as taciturnity in its implications.
C. a mark of intelligence.
D. an indirect cause of taciturnity.
E. a possible indication of maladjustment.

64.3
DETAIL

The high value which our culture places on volubility is
A. felt by the author to be the cause of a good deal of harm.
B. cited by the author as a sound reason for cultivating the ability to speak extemporaneously.
C. a result of the common belief that people who talk little are maladjusted.
D. cited by the author to justify why schools and universities emphasize speech courses.
E. a reason why everyone in our culture talks more than he should.

64.4
SIGNIFICANCE

The writer feels that evidence of glibness in an individual should be
A. praised.   D. encouraged.
B. evaluated.   E. ignored.
C. discouraged.

64.5
CONCLUSION

The writer appears to favor verbal reactions which are
A. glib.   D. sparse.
B. relatively quiet. E. immediate.
C. deliberate.

64.9
COMMUNICATION TECHNIQUE

The author attempts to establish his thesis in this passage by
A. citing cases.
B. unsupported statements with which the reader may agree.
C. logical reasoning.
D. contrast and comparison.
E. clinical explanation of the effects of glibness.

65

As we know the short story today it is largely a product of the nineteenth and twentieth centuries, and its development parallels the rapid development of industrialism in America. We have been a busy people, busy principally in evolving a production system supremely efficient. Railroads and factories have blossomed almost overnight; mines and oil fields have been discovered and exploited; mechanical inventions by the thousand have been made and perfected. Speed has been an essential element in our endeavors, and it has affected our lives, our very natures. Leisurely reading has been, for most Americans, impossible. As with our meals, we have grabbed bits of reading standing up, cafeteria style, and gulped down cups of sentiment on the run. We have had to read while hanging onto a strap in a swaying trolley car or in a rushing subway or while tending to a clamoring telephone switchboard. Our popular magazine has been our literary **automat**, and its stories have often been no more substantial than sandwiches.

────────────────── Questions for Passage #65 ──────────────────

65.5
CONCLUSION

The writer's purpose in discussing the short story is primarily to
A. praise it.
B. show his disapproval.
C. explain how it came about.
D. explain its technique.
E. use it as an example of how busy Americans have become.

65.8
VOCABULARY

In comparing the popular magazine to an "automat," the author is emphasizing the fact that its contents are
A. conveniently available.
B. repetitive in nature.
C. inexpensive.
D. presented in great variety.
E. the result of large publishing resources.

65.9
COMMUNICATION
TECHNIQUE

The author presents his generalization by the use of
A. several vivid similes.
B. several vivid metaphors.
C. a literal recital of facts.
D. a series of statements, each of which is supported by evidence to prove it.
E. facts from which conclusions are drawn.

66

There is a time in every man's education when he arrives at the conviction that envy is ignorance; that imitation is suicide; that he must take himself for better or for worse as his portion; that though the wide universe is full of good, no kernel of nourishing corn can come to him but through his toil bestowed on **that plot of ground which is given to him to till.** The power which resides in him is new in nature, and none but he knows what that is which he can do, nor does he know until he has tried.

66.4
SIGNIFICANCE

Essentially, the reader of this passage is advised to

A. know himself.

B. learn from others.

C. limit his aspiration to goals which he has demonstrated are feasible.

D. work hard.

E. stop his education and go out into the practical world.

66.7
TONE

The author of this passage is apparently

A. self-contradictory.

B. confused about what he believes.

C. non-conformist.

D. sanguine and non-conformist.

E. didactic, sanguine, and non-conformist.

66.8
VOCABULARY

By his reference to "that plot of ground which is given to him to till" the author refers to

A. a piece of land which one might own.

B. the power of nature which man can tap.

C. one's portion of wealth gained by one's own toil.

D. one's own talents.

E. a place for growing nourishing corn.

67

Shakespeare is thus continually reminding us of our own experiences and expressing them for us. Moreover, as we grow older and the range of our experience widens, so his range grows, too. He is always giving us back our own, so that we understand his plays more and ourselves better. The reward of the study of literature is that we are constantly deepening our own experience and understanding, and of all English literature the study of Shakespeare is the most valuable. It gives us the power of detaching ourselves from ourselves and seeing our own lives as part of universal life, as players playing out our own seven acts on the universal stage, and at the same time enjoying the experience of the play as players on the stage and as critics in the audience.

67.1
SUBJECT MATTER

This passage primarily treats

A. the rewards of literature.

B. the value of the study of Shakespeare.

C. how Shakespeare enables us to be both actors and critics.

D. of Shakespeare's help in getting us to see ourselves as part of universal life.

E. ways we can develop self-awareness.

67.3 (a)
DETAIL

The author says that as we grow older,
A. Shakespeare adds valuable experiences to our own.
B. Shakespeare's plays become more complicated.
C. Shakespeare reminds us of our experience.
D. Shakespeare's plays become richer for us.
E. we are able to respond to a greater number of Shakespeare's plays.

67.3 (b)
DETAIL

The study of Shakespeare, according to the author, gives us the power to
A. thoroughly enjoy the experience of a play as detached observers.
B. become actors in the world drama.
C. share our experiences with others.
D. enjoy plays through reading rather than by attending a theatre.
E. stand off and observe ourselves as part of the life of the whole world.

67.5
CONCLUSION

The author's purpose in writing this passage is to
A. interest us in the study of Shakespeare.
B. show us Shakespeare was a genius.
C. show how Shakespeare was different from other dramatists.
D. show how Shakespeare influences our lives.
E. get us to respect Shakespeare.

67.9
COMMUNICATION
TECHNIQUE

The distinction the author makes between Shakespeare's plays and other literature is
A. a distinction without a difference.
B. proved by the details about Shakespeare which follow it in the passage.
C. proved by the details about Shakespeare which precede it in the passage.
D. proved by all the statements made about Shakespeare's great value.
E. unsupported by proof.

68

A hundred years ago, when there were only half as many inhabitants in Europe, the best minds shared the gloomy view of Thomas Robert Malthus. He believed that human population always increases faster than the food supply and that misery and want and war are the inevitable consequences. Three hundred years ago, when the population was about the same as it had been for thousands of years, famine was a periodic experience which came so regularly that people accepted it as normal, like the succession of the seasons. "Seven famines and ten years of famine in a century" was the "law regulating scarcities" prior to 1600, and it was accepted in Malthus's day as some now accept the "law of business cycles."

68.2
GENERALIZATION

Which of the following most correctly summarizes the main idea of the passage?

A. A hundred years ago, when there were only half as many inhabitants in Europe, the best minds shared the gloomy view of Thomas Robert Malthus.

B. Three hundred years ago famine was a periodic experience which came so regularly that men accepted it as normal, like the successions of the seasons.

C. Men tend to accept the economic conditions of their time as instances of economic laws.

D. Seven famines and ten years of famine in a century was the law regulating scarcities prior to 1600, and men accepted it as some now accept the "law of business cycles."

E. Malthus believed that the human population always increases faster than the food supply and misery and want and war are the inevitable consequences.

68.3
DETAIL

Malthus's theory was accepted because

A. people were more ignorant in Malthus's time.

B. it made some people rich.

C. it was an excuse for wars.

D. famine was felt to be normal.

E. Europe was overpopulated.

68.4
SIGNIFICANCE

The author of this passage would most probably expect the reader to

A. agree with Malthus's views.

B. be grateful for the improvement in man's lot over the past three centuries.

C. find out what views are accepted by today's best minds.

D. reject the concept that man's economy cannot be modified.

E. do none of the above.

68.5 (a)
CONCLUSION

Malthus's theory was

A. discouraging.

B. contradictory.

C. unjustified by the conditions of the day.

D. inspiring.

E. little known.

68.5 (b)
CONCLUSION

The author implies that Malthus's theory

A. was contrary to fact.

B. is not accepted by modern thinkers.

C. caused famines.

D. is undeniably true.

E. has been proven by verifiable evidence.

68.6
APPLICATION

Malthus would probably have supported

A. farm subsidies.

B. the United Nations as an instrument to avoid war.

C. a minimum wage and hour law.

D. graduated income tax to redistribute wealth.

E. none of the above.

Man is an inventive creature and an imitative one. He has always loved to mimic his fellows, and it is a short step from mimic representations to making stories and poems which imitate human actions and passions. His pleasure in mimicry and story telling is paralleled by his love of seeing pantomimic actions and in hearing or reading stories and lyrics. This pleasure in inventing fictions and in listening to the inventions of others is the source of the immense body of literature which, in this text, we shall call poetry, or poetic literature. Our use of the word *poetry*, while it is by no means new, is not commonly employed today; for poetry, to most people, signifies literature which is written in verse, especially verse that conforms to recognizable metrical patterns. This meaning of poetry is, however, a very limited one. It defines literary works in terms of techniques in the use of the language rather than in terms of ends which they serve. A few histories and philosophical works have been written in verse. Novels, dramas, short stories, and lyrics, whether written in prose or verse, have this in common: they are representations of human experience, the purpose of which is to give pleasure, the pleasure of each being appropriate to the kind of representation. To designate such works as creative or imaginative literature would imply that the production of histories and philosophical works did not involve creative or imaginative effort. In the absence of a better word and because there is historical precedent for it, we shall use the term *poetry* to designate all literature which is written in response to the human need to express through imitation our sensitivity to the actions, thoughts, and passions of men.

—————————————————— Questions for Passage #69 ——————————————————

**69.2
GENERALIZATION**

Poetic literature, as the author conceives it, arises most directly from man's

A. need for history and philosophy.
B. need for rhythm.
C. pleasure in mimicry.
D. love of reading.
E. actions, thoughts, and passions.

**69.3
DETAIL**

The author of this passage feels that the designation of literature as "poetical" only when it is written in verse

A. is acceptable because it is technically correct.
B. excludes many historical and philosophical works which would otherwise be so designated.
C. is historically justified.
D. ignores the intent of the author.
E. is none of these things.

**69.9
COMMUNICATION
TECHNIQUE**

The author's method of presenting his contention is one of

A. inductive reasoning from specific examples.
B. analogy.
C. anecdote and incident.
D. comparison and contrast.
E. definition and logical reasoning.

This change of human disposition toward the world does not mean that man ceases to have ideals, or ceases to be primarily a creature of the imagination. But it does signify a radical change in the character and function of the ideal realm which man shapes for himself. In the classic philosophy, the ideal world is essentially a haven in which man finds rest from the storm of life; it is an asylum in which he takes refuge from the troubles of existence with the calm assurance that it alone is supremely real. When the belief that knowledge is active and operative takes hold of men, the ideal realm is no longer something aloof and separate; it is rather that collection of imagined possibilities that stimulates men to new efforts and realizations. It still remains true that the troubles which men undergo are the forces that lead them to project pictures of a better state of things. But the picture of the better is shaped so that it may become an instrumentality of action, while in the classic view the idea belongs ready-made in a noumenal world. . . . .

—————————— Questions for Passage #70 ——————————

**70.1
SUBJECT MATTER**

This passage is about

A. the contrast between the old and new ideal worlds.
B. the change in people's dispositions since the modern era.
C. how man deals with his difficulties.
D. the nature of man's ideal world.
E. the function of the ideal world.

**70.2
GENERALIZATION**

The main thought of this passage is that

A. man's attitude toward the world has become more aggressive and less idealistic.
B. the ideal world which man can imagine today is one of possibilities for betterment rather than a haven for refuge.
C. man has jettisoned the classic view of the world as static and antagonistic.
D. both the classic and the modern concepts of the ideal world are based upon the realization that man's efforts at improvement are the results of his trouble in the real world.
E. none of the above is true.

**70.3
DETAIL**

Men who have the modern approach to an ideal world feel that

A. their ideals are merely creations of imagination and are not real.
B. they are better off without ideals.
C. their ideals are goads to action.
D. such an approach helps them to feel secure.
E. such an approach points to radicalism as a way of life.

**70.6
APPLICATION**

According to the passage, it is probable that Plato, the Athenian philosopher who wrote of the first perfect state in his *Republic*, felt that

A. his imagined country was more real than Athens itself.
B. his work was a design for the improvement of the state.
C. it was drawn from Athenian life and showed little creative imagination.
D. his creation would die with him.
E. the picture he drew would inspire Athenians to be better people.

There is a great, silent conspiracy between us to forget death; all our lives are spent in busily forgetting death. That is why we are active about so many things which we know to be unimportant; why we are so afraid of solitude, and so thankful for the company of our fellow-creatures. Allowing ourselves, for the most part, to be but vaguely conscious of that great suspense in which we live, we find our escape from its sterile, annihilating reality in many dreams, in religion, passion, art; each a forgetfulness, each a symbol of creation; religion being the creation of a new heaven, passion a creation of a new earth, and art, in its mingling of heaven and earth, the creation of heaven out of earth. Each is a kind of sublime selfishness, the saint, the lover, and the artist having each an **incommunicable** ecstasy which he esteems as his ultimate attainment, however, in his lower moments, he may serve God in action, or do the will of his mistress, or minister to men by showing them a little beauty. But it is before all things, an escape; and the prophets who have redeemed the world, and the artists who have made the world beautiful, and the lovers who have quickened the pulses of the world, have really whether they knew it or not, been fleeing from the certainty of one thought: that we have all of us, only our one day; and from the dread of that other thought: that the day, however used, must after all be wasted.

─────────────── Questions for Passage #71 ───────────────

71.2
GENERALIZATION

The author's main thought is that human action is motivated chiefly by desire to
A. create works of art to make us immortal.
B. escape the knowledge of death.
C. fulfill selfish desires no matter how laudable they may appear.
D. serve God.
E. face death's sterile reality.

71.5
CONCLUSION

The author links together the artist, the lover, and the religious man because each
A. is aware of death.
B. is selfish.
C. must sooner or later die.
D. gives a little beauty to the world and quickens its pulse.
E. is involved in creative effort to escape the thought of death.

71.7
TONE

The tone of this passage is
A. optimistic.
B. pessimistic.
C. sentimental.
D. coldly factual.
E. sarcastic.

71.8
VOCABULARY

An "incommunicable" ecstacy is
A. unsurpassable.
B. greedy.
C. unexpressible.
D. solitary.
E. non-transferable.

As a result of the separation from Great Britain by the colonies acting as a unit, the powers of external sovereignty passed from the Crown not to the colonies severally, but to the colonies in their collective and corporate capacity as the United States of America. Even before the Declaration, the colonies were a unit in foreign affairs, acting through a common agency — namely the Continental Congress, composed of delegates from the thirteen colonies. That agency exercised the powers of war and peace, raised an army, created a navy, and finally adopted the Declaration of Independence. Rulers come and go; governments and the forms of government change; but sovereignty survives. A political society cannot endure without a supreme will somewhere. Sovereignty is never held in suspense. When, therefore, the external sovereignty of Great Britain in respect of the colonies ceased, it immediately passed to the Union. That fact was given practical application almost at once. The treaty of peace, made on September 23, 1783, was concluded between his Britannic Majesty and the "United States of America."

The Union existed before the Constitution, which was ordained and established among other things to form "a more perfect Union." Prior to that event, it is clear that the Union, declared by the Articles of Confederation to be "perpetual," was the sole possessor of external sovereignty, and in the Union it remained without change save in so far as the Constitution in express terms qualified its exercise. The Framers' Convention was called and exerted its powers upon the irrefutable postulate that though the states were several, their people in respect of foreign affairs were one. In that convention, the entire absence of state power to deal with those affairs was thus forcefully stated by Rufus King:

> The states were not "sovereigns" in the sense contended for by some. They did not possess the peculiar features of sovereignty, — they could not make war, nor peace, nor alliances, nor treaties. Considering them as political beings, they were dumb, for they could not speak to any foreign sovereign whatever. They were deaf, for they could not hear any propositions from such sovereign. They had not even the organs or faculties of defense or offense, for they could not of themselves raise troops, or equip vessels, for war.

It results that the investment of the federal government with the powers of external sovereignty did not depend upon the affirmative grants of the Constitution. The powers to declare and wage war, to conclude peace, to make treaties, to maintain diplomatic relations with other sovereignties, if they had never been mentioned in the Constitution, would have vested in the federal government as necessary concomitants of nationality. Neither the Constitution nor the laws passed in pursuance of it have any force in foreign territory unless in respect of our own citizens; and operations of the nation in such territory must be governed by treaties, international understandings and compacts, and the principles of international law. As a member of the family of nations, the right and power of the United States in that field are equal to the right and power of the other members of the international family. Otherwise, the United States is not completely sovereign. The power to acquire territory by discovery and occupation, the power to expel undesirable aliens, the power to make such international agreements as do not constitute treaties in the constitutional sense, none of which is expressly affirmed by the Constitution, nevertheless exist as inherently inseparable from the conception of nationality. This the court recognized, and in each of the cases cited found the warrant for its conclusions not in the provisions of the Constitution, but in the law of nations.

————————————————— Questions for Passage #72 —————————————————

**72.1
SUBJECT MATTER**

Which of the following would be the best title for the passage?
A. Sovereignty Among Nations
B. The Constitutional Basis of Sovereignty
C. The Nature of Sovereignty in United States Government
D. The Implications of the Constitution in International Affairs
E. The Subtleties of the Constitution in Regard to Sovereignty

**72.2
GENERALIZATION**

The main idea of this passage is that
A. the power of the U.S. to make treaties, expel undesirable aliens, make war, etc., derives from the provisions of the Constitution.
B. the states do not have sovereign power because they are smaller and less wealthy and powerful than the Federal government.
C. the power of the United States to act as a sovereign existed before the Constitution.
D. the United States' sovereign power derives from its existence as a nation.
E. other nations have granted sovereign power to the United States.

**72.6 (a)
APPLICATION**

According to this passage, which of the following pairs are permitted to enter into treaties?
A. New York and Canada.
B. Philadelphia and Pennsylvania.
C. United States and Mexico.
D. New Jersey and Delaware.
E. California and San Diego.

**72.6 (b)
APPLICATION**

To which of the following situations could the passage be directed?
A. The Continental Congress wishes to repeal the Constitution.
B. The power to declare war has not been granted by the Constitution to the House of Representatives, but the House declares war.
C. New York enters into a treaty with Connecticut which New Jersey doesn't like.
D. An alien deemed undesirable by the U.S. government does not wish to be expelled from the country.
E. Rufus King forcefully attempts to form his own sovereignty.

12

The Hanging Gardens, or the Gardens of Semiramis, as they were sometimes called, rose from a river in the north of Babylon in a series of terraces, or "setbacks," which were provided with earth deep enough to accommodate trees of great size. Ancient writers tell us that the lavish King Nebuchadnessar built this skyscraper of foliage to gratify his wife Amytis, who had been raised among the hills of Media. She soon wearied of the flat plains of Babylon, so her husband, **solicitous** of her well-being, ordered the gardens erected to remind his homesick queen of her native hills.

_____ Questions for Passage #73 _____

73.1
SUBJECT MATTER

The purpose of the author in writing this passage is to tell us about
A. the relationship of Nebuchadnezzar and Amytis.
B. the nature and genesis of the Gardens of Semiramis.
C. the method of construction of the Hanging Gardens.
D. the character of Nebuchadnezzar.
E. the way the Hanging Gardens came about.

73.2
GENERALIZATION

The main thought of this passage is that the Hanging Gardens were
A. the world's first skyscraper.
B. man-made.
C. ancient.
D. a series of artificially built up terraces with earth deep enough to hold big trees.
E. built because King Nebuchadnezzar wanted to please his wife.

73.3
DETAIL

The Hanging Gardens consisted of artificially constructed terraces of earth on which all types of foliage were planted. These terraces were built
A. in the south of Babylon.
B. only in the minds of ancient writers.
C. near Queen Amytis' native hills.
D. where the flat plains of Babylon met the hills of Media.
E. next to a river in Babylon.

73.8
VOCABULARY

If the King was "solicitous of her well-being," he was
A. determined to impress her.
B. afraid to cross her.
C. seeking to increase her love for him.
D. trying to divert her.
E. concerned about her peace of mind.

The attitude of the teacher toward her pupils does much to form the opinion that they have of themselves. If she expresses faith in her pupils, recognizes their strong points, and adjusts the work to their capacities, she is apt to condition them to have desirable attitudes about themselves and their work. On the other hand, if she displays contempt for their abilities, minimizes their efforts, and is inflexible in her requirements, she will help develop associations that may give rise to unhappy emotional states. When these associations come to mind, the emotions surrounding them will be reinstated. The emotions may be either **invigorating** or depressing.

_____ Questions for Passage #74 _____

**74.1
SUBJECT MATTER**

This passage is chiefly concerned with showing
A. why students fail.
B. how students associate a subject with the teacher who teaches it.
C. how important is the emotional aspect of learning.
D. the differences between good and bad teachers.
E. the effect of teachers' attitudes on students' self-concepts.

**74.2
GENERALIZATION**

The main thought of this paragraph is that
A. the teacher should express faith in her students, recognize strong points, and adjust the work to their capabilities.
B. the teacher may make pupils unhappy by minimizing their efforts, and being too rigid in her requirements.
C. students' work in class is accompanied by emotional states, which may be invigorating or depressing.
D. it is the job of the teacher to so teach that children enjoy their school work.
E. the teacher's attitude toward her pupils helps form the pupils' attitudes and emotions.

**74.5
CONCLUSION**

We can conclude from the passage that a student's attitude toward a subject is most strongly influenced by
A. the student's likes and dislikes of the subject itself.
B. the teacher's likes or dislikes about the subject.
C. the teacher's reactions to the student.
D. the teacher's reactions to the student's performance.
E. the student's capacity for emotional control.

**74.7
TONE**

The passage describes two types of teachers. The author seems to
A. condemn the inflexible teacher.
B. approve of the teacher who has faith in her students.
C. have not made up his mind on his preference for either.
D. feel that it is the student who determines his own success.
E. be scientifically objective about them.

**74.8
VOCABULARY**

By "invigorating" the author means most nearly
A. stimulating.   D. healthful.
B. easily recalled.   E. recurring.
C. negative.

What we see when we photograph the Sun is a huge glowing ball of gas. Underneath this hot and extremely bright photosphere lies other gas while, in the central parts of the Sun, atoms are continually being broken down and built up. In the center of the Sun it is just as if hundreds of thousands of hydrogen bombs were continually exploding, and the results of this reach the photosphere. This is why the photosphere shines so brightly and sends out x-rays and ultra-violet light. Yet sometimes dark spots appear on the photosphere and these 'sunspots' are evidence of greatly increased activity below. When sunspots appear, great bursts of the longer radio waves are often received. These are a thousand times more intense than those which radio-astronomers normally receive and which come from what is called the 'quiet' Sun, being radiated by the corona and the 'chromosphere,' that layer of not very bright gas which lies just above the photosphere. These immense bursts of radio waves are usually accompanied by an intensely bright area of 'flare' near a sunspot, and it is clear that they are caused by a sudden burst of thermal radiation from below the photosphere. The visible flare and the burst of radio waves are also accompanied by a burst of x-rays, ultra-violet rays, and atomic particles.

When there are sunspots but no flares accompanying them, the radio waves emitted by the 'quiet' Sun do not remain constant but begin to fluctuate, and the radio signals gradually become stronger. These changes do not correlate with changes in the number of sunspots, although it has been found that the radio waves seem to be generated in the Sun's atmosphere *above* the sunspots and not in the sunspots themselves. The changes in radio signals do, however, correlate with the calcium areas of the Sun's spectrum.

Radio astronomy has helped considerably to increase our knowledge of the corona. Being visually very dim, the corona is hard to observe by optical means, even during total eclipses. During some eclipses it has been traced quite a long way from the Sun but was believed to extend no more than about two million miles at the most above the photosphere. Direct radiation of radio waves from the corona have been received during daylight up to about 1½ million miles. However, by examining a distant radio source as the Sun passes in front of it, it is possible to discover how far the corona extends by observing how the radio waves from the distant source are affected. It was in this way that Professors M. Ryle and A. Hewish at Cambridge University, England, found that the corona could be traced out to more than 6 million miles, and in the line of the Sun's equator to 12 million miles or more. It has even been suggested that the corona extends as far as the Earth itself.

75.1
SUBJECT MATTER

A good title for this selection would be:
A. What Radio Astronomy Tells Us About the Sun.
B. Radio Astronomy.
C. Sunspots.
D. Facts About the Sun's Corona.
E. The Nature of the Sun.

75.3 (a)
DETAIL

From the center out, the correct order of the sun's layers is
A. photosphere, corona, chromosphere.
B. spectrum, chromosphere, photosphere, corona.
C. chromosphere, photosphere, spectrum, corona.
D. corona, photosphere, chromosphere.
E. photosphere, chromosphere, corona.

75.3 (b)
DETAIL

The photosphere is the
A. part of the sun we usually see.
B. layer of gas which forms the corona.
C. area in the sun where atoms break down and build up.
D. area of the sun which sends out radio waves.
E. part of the sun which reflects the calcium areas of the sun's spectrum.

75.3 (c)
DETAIL

One bit of knowledge gained from radio astronomy which the passage does *not* mention is information dealing with the
A. nuclear activity in the center of the sun.
B. intensity of ultra-violet rays in the earth's atmosphere.
C. activity of the chromosphere.
D. extent of the corona.
E. "quiet" sun.

75.5
CONCLUSION

Professors M. Ryle and A. Hewish have found that the sun's corona
A. extends as far as the earth itself.
B. can be measured by noting its effect on radio waves passing through it.
C. extends not more than two million miles above the photosphere.
D. gives off x-rays.
E. is easily observed by astronomers.

76

I can remember the bare wooden stairway in my uncle's house, and the turn to the left above the landing, and the slanting roof over my bed, and the squares of moonlight on the floor, and the white cold world of snow outside, seen through the curtainless window. I can remember the howling of the wind and the quaking of the house on stormy nights, and how snug and cozy one felt, under the blankets, listening, and how the powdery snow used to sift in, around the sashes, and lie in little ridges on the floor and make the place look chilly in the morning and curb the wild desire to get up — in case there was any. I can remember how very dark that room was, in the dark of the moon, and how packed it was with ghostly stillness when one woke up by accident away in the night, and forgotten sins came flocking out of the secret chambers of the memory and wanted a hearing; and how dismal was the hoo-hooing of the owl and the wailing of the wolf, sent mourning by on the night wind.

Go on to next page. ➤

76.5
CONCLUSION

The boy in this passage is recalling nights in his uncle's house that were
A. still and cold and snowy.
B. spent in the cozy surroundings of a well-furnished home.
C. filled with the noises of city traffic.
D. clear, cold, and windy.
E. wintry and cloudy.

76.7
TONE

The author describes his uncle's house to
A. create of mood of nostalgia.
B. entertain us with the quaintness of early Americana.
C. delight us with reminiscences.
D. delineate the terrors of night as seen by a young boy.
E. show us the horror of his youth.

77

Producing his papers, he pointed out the great contrast between the number of deaths per annum in the small town near London where he lived, and the number of deaths per annum in a low district of London — Bermondsey, or Lambeth, or some region on the Surreyside. On this great contrast he triumphantly **dilated**, as proving how much could be done by good drainage, ventilation, and so on. On the one hand, he passed over the fact that his suburban place was, in large measure, inhabited by a picked population — people of means, well fed and clothed, able to secure all appliances for comfort, leading regular lives, free from overwork and anxiety. On the other hand, he passed over the fact that this low region of London was, by virtue of its lowness, one out of which all citizens **pecuniarily** able to take care of themselves escaped if they could, and into which were thrust great numbers whose poverty excluded them from better regions — the ill-fed, the drunken, the dissolute, and others on the highway to death. Though, in the first place, the healthiness of the locality obviously drew to it an excess of persons likely to live long; and though, in the second case, the unhealthiness of the locality made it one in which an excess of those not likely to live long were left to dwell, or to hide themselves to die; yet the whole difference was put down to direct effects of pure air and impure air respectively.

77.2
GENERALIZATION

The author's purpose in this passage is to show that
A. the speaker has not proved that physical improvements caused a decline in the death rate.
B. the speaker left out important factors affecting the death rate.
C. it is difficult, if not impossible, to determine clearly the controlling factors affecting death rates.
D. London is not significantly less healthful than small towns near London.
E. death rates depend on moral rather than physical factors.

77.6
APPLICATION

According to the author of this passage, its subject would be likely to

A. look to explanations of the differences in the degree of success of various social classes in the heredity of the individuals making up such classes.

B. really believe that the average family has 2.5 children.

C. make a good health commissioner because of his sincere interest in the health of citizens.

D. feel that "lies and statistics" have a good deal in common.

E. conclude that, because the figures relating to numbers of persons hospitalized for mental diseases show increases for each year since 1910, civilization is getting "sicker."

77.8 (a)
VOCABULARY

The meaning of the word "dilated" can best be rendered as

A. explained.　　　　　D. swelled.

B. expanded.　　　　　E. concluded.

C. observed.

77.8 (b)
VOCABULARY

People "pecuniarily" able to take care of themselves are

A. resourceful.　　　　D. aggressive.

B. intelligent.　　　　E. healthy.

C. self-supporting.

77.9
COMMUNICATION
TECHNIQUE

The fact that those financially able to escape the low part of London did so is cited as proof that

A. economic conditions in London were improving.

B. poverty is synonymous with ill health.

C. the low part was unhealthful.

D. those who remained were of low moral character.

E. good housing accommodations were unavailable to those who could afford them.

78

With a view of causing an increase to take place in the mass of national wealth, . . . the general rule is, that nothing ought to be done or attempted by government. The motto, or watchword of government on these occasions, ought to be — "Be Quiet." For this quietism there are two main reasons: 1. Generally speaking, any interference for this purpose on the part of the government is "needless" . . . There is no one who knows what is for your interest, so well as yourself — no one who is disposed with so much ardor and constancy to pursue it. 2. Generally speaking, it is moreover likely to be **pernicious,** *viz.*, by being unconductive, or even obstructive, with reference to the attainment of the end in view. It is, moreover, universally and constantly pernicious in another way, by the restraint or constraint imposed on the free agency of the individual. Pain is the general concomitant of the sense of such restraint, wherever it is experienced. . . . With few exceptions, and those not very considerable ones, the attainment of the maximum enjoyment will be most effectually secured by leaving each individual to pursue his own maximum of enjoyment, in proportion as he is in possession of the means . . . . The art, therefore, is reduced within small compass: "security" and "freedom" are all that industry requires. The request which agriculture, manufacturers, and commerce present to governments is modest and reasonable as that which Diogenes made to Alexander: "Stand out of my sunshine." We have no need of favor — we require only a secure and open path.

Go on to next page. ➤

78.4
SIGNIFICANCE

The author is most concerned with having government
A. give security to industry by passing laws subsidizing it.
B. improve its insight into the problems of industry.
C. trust people to further their own interests.
D. pass laws to secure an increase of national wealth.
E. cease to interfere in the affairs of industry.

78.6 (a)
APPLICATION

The author would be apt to be in favor of
A. farm subsidies.   D. excess profits taxes.
B. social security legislation.   E. none of the above.
C. labor unions.

78.6 (b)
APPLICATION

The policy advocated by the author in this passage is known as
A. laissez faire.   D. Machiavellianism.
B. separation of church and state.   E. peaceful coexistence.
C. mercantilism.

78.8
VOCABULARY

As used in this passage, "pernicious" means
A. persistent.   D. harmful.
B. confusing.   E. foolish.
C. unproductive.

78.9
COMMUNICATION
TECHNIQUE

The author's citation of Diogenes' request to Alexander the Great is an example of
A. an appeal to those with classical educations to identify with the author.
B. use of a simile.
C. proof by historical precedent.
D. a humorous reference to lighten a serious argument.
E. reasoning by analogy.

79

The rating assigned to an I.Q. depends upon the test from which it was derived. For most current intelligence scales the I.Q. range 90-110 includes approximately 50 percent of the population and is accordingly interpreted as representing average intelligence. I.Q.'s of 110-120, which include some 16 percent, are classified as bright normal; I.Q.'s of 120-130 (about 7 percent) as superior; and I.Q.'s over 130, the top 2 percent, as very superior. Comparably, I.Q.'s of 80-90 (approximately 16 percent) are classified as dull normal; I.Q.'s of 70-80 (6 percent) as borderline, and I.Q.'s below 70 (2-3 percent) are usually considered mentally retarded or defective. These limits are only approximate; other factors have to be taken into consideration when classifying a person.

79.1
SUBJECT MATTER

The best title for this selection would be:
A. Rate Your I.Q.
B. I.Q. Ratings.
C. Superior and Retarded Minds.
D. How Much Can We Expect From People?
E. Average Intelligence.

79.3
DETAIL

An I.Q. of 74 would, on most current intelligence scales, classify an individual as

A. mentally defective.
B. dull normal.
C. 6 percent below dull normal.
D. borderline between dull normal and mentally retarded.
E. none of the above.

79.4
SIGNIFICANCE

The author states that persons engaged in rating a person's intelligence should

A. simply follow the scales set forth in the passage.
B. always use the same test.
C. not rely solely upon intelligence tests.
D. avoid borderline scores as confusing.
E. do none of the above.

79.6
APPLICATION

If an I.Q. of 110 or better is desirable as minimum equipment for college work, and 1,000,000 persons graduate from high school in a given year, how many would you expect to be excluded from college, other factors not controlling your calculations?

A. 100,000
B. 160,000
C. 250,000
D. 500,000
E. 750,000

80

As one works with color in a practical or experimental way, one is impressed by two apparently unrelated facts. Color as seen is a mobile changeable thing depending to a large extent on the relationship of the color to other colors seen simultaneously. It is not fixed in its relation to the direct stimulus which creates it. On the other hand, the properties of surfaces that give rise to color do not seem to change greatly under a wide variety of illumination colors, usually (but not always) looking much the same in artificial light as in daylight. Both of these effects seem to be due in large part to the mechanism of color adaptation mentioned earlier.

When the eye is fixed on a colored area, there is an immediate readjustment of the sensitivity of the eye to color in and around the area viewed. This readjustment does not immediately affect the color seen but usually does affect the next area to which the gaze is shifted. The longer the time of viewing, the higher the intensity, and the larger the area, the greater the effect will be in terms of its persistence in the succeeding viewing situation. As indicated by the work of Wright and Schouten, it appears that, at least for a first approximation, full adaptation takes place over a very brief time if the adapting source is moderately bright and the eye has been in relative darkness just previously. As the stimulus is allowed to act, however, the effect becomes more *persistent* in the sense that it takes the eye longer to regain its sensitivity to lower intensities. The net result is that, if the eye is so exposed and then the gaze is transferred to an area of *lower* intensity, the loss of sensitivity produced by the first area will still be present and appear as an "afterimage" superimposed on the second. The effect not only is present over the actual area causing the "local adaptation" but also spreads with decreasing strength to adjoining areas of the eye to produce "lateral adaptation." Also, because of the persistence of the effect if the eye is shifted around from one object to another, all of which are at similar brightnesses or have similar colors, the adaptation will tend to become uniform over the whole eye.

Go on to next page. ➤

80.1
SUBJECT MATTER

This selection is concerned primarily with
A. the eye's adaptation to color.
B. the properties of colored surfaces.
C. the color of colors.
D. the effect of changes in color intensity.
E. none of these subjects.

80.2
GENERALIZATION

Whether a colored object would, on two viewings separated in time, appear to the viewer as similar or different in color would depend mostly on
A. the color mechanism of the eye in use at the time of each viewing.
B. what kind of viewing had immediately preceded each of the viewings.
C. the properties of the surface being viewed.
D. the individual's power of lateral adaptation.
E. whether the object was seen in artificial or natural light.

80.6
APPLICATION

If a person's eye has been looking at an object in bright sunlight for some time, and then shifts to an object not well lit — such as a lawn or shrub in shadow — we can expect
A. a time lag in the focusing ability of the eye.
B. some inability to see colors of the latter-named objects until loss of sensitivity has been regained.
C. the immediate loss of the "afterimage" of the first object.
D. adaptation in the central area of the eye but little adaptation in the lateral areas to the new intensity level.
E. none of these to be true.

80.9
COMMUNICATION TECHNIQUE

The present selection has apparently been preceded by some explanation of
A. some experiments with color pigments.
B. the nature of color.
C. the color properties of various surfaces.
D. the mechanism of the eye's adaptation to color.
E. none of these subjects.

81

The change in the treatment of his characters is a significant index to Shakespeare's growth as a dramatist. In the earlier plays, his men and women are more engaged with external forces than with internal struggles. In as excellent an early tragedy as "Romeo and Juliet," the hero fights more with outside obstacles than with himself. In the great later tragedies, the **internal conflict** is more emphasized, as in the cases of "Hamlet" and "Macbeth." He grew to care less for mere incident, for plots based on mistaken identity, as in the "Comedy of Errors"; he became more and more interested in the delineation of character, in showing the effect of evil on Macbeth and his wife, of jealousy on Othello, of indecision on Hamlet, as well as in exploring the ineffectual attempts of many of his characters to escape the consequences of their acts.

81.3 (a)
DETAIL

In his later plays Shakespeare became more interested in
A. plots based on mistaken identity.
B. great characters from history.
C. the study of his country.
D. the study of human nature.
E. the struggle of the hero with external forces.

81.3 (b)
DETAIL

The development of Shakespeare as a dramatist is marked by his
A. improved treatment of complications.
B. increased use of involved plots.
C. increased variety of plots.
D. decreased dependency on historical characters.
E. increased interest in emotional conflicts.

81.5
CONCLUSION

The author feels that growth on the part of a dramatist includes an increased ability to
A. explore human nature.
B. weave engrossing plots.
C. show the helplessness of man in his confrontation with his environment.
D. master the technique of the stage.
E. change his approach.

81.6
APPLICATION

The growth referred to in question 81.3 (b) should lead us to expect greater evidence in his later plays of
A. rapid shifts of scenery.
B. soliloquies.
C. low comedy.
D. alarums and excursions.
E. none of these.

81.8
VOCABULARY

By "internal conflict" the author has in mind conflicts arising from
A. fights among families.
B. fights between enemies.
C. difficulties brought upon the characters by an unfortunate destiny.
D. the characters of his protagonists.
E. difficulties within himself that Shakespeare probably experienced in his own life.

81.9
COMMUNICATION
TECHNIQUE

The author develops his GENERALIZATION in this passage through the use of
A. inductive reasoning from facts.
B. analogy.
C. logical reasoning from a premise.
D. negative arguments.
E. contrast.

Nationalism is not a harmonious natural growth, qualitatively identical with the love for family and home. It is frequently assumed that man loves in widening circles — his family, his village, his tribe or clan, the nation, and finally humanity and the supreme good. But love of home and family is a concrete feeling, accessible to everyone in daily experience, while nationalism, and in an even higher degree cosmopolitanism, is a highly complex and originally an abstract feeling. Nationalism — our identification with the life and aspirations of uncounted millions whom we shall never know, with a territory which we shall never visit in its entirety — is **qualitatively** different from love of family or of home surroundings. It is qualitatively akin to the love of humanity or of the whole earth.

_____ Questions for Passage #82 _____

82.1
SUBJECT MATTER

A good title for this passage would be:
A. A Distinction Without a Difference.
B. Love of One's Fellow Beings.
C. The Nature of Nationalism.
D. An Abstract Affection.
E. Our Complex Emotions.

82.2 (a)
GENERALIZATION

Compared with nationalism, love of home and family is more
A. conclusive.
B. complex.
C. difficult to attain.
D. abstract.
E. concrete.

82.2 (b)
GENERALIZATION

A common assumption regarding nationalism is that it is
A. more nearly related to humanity than to the home.
B. identified with the lives of millions whom we do not know.
C. highly abstract and complex.
D. stimulated by travel within one's own country.
E. an outgrowth of love of home and family.

82.6
APPLICATION

If the author's contention about an individual's loyalties is true, it would require the greatest intellectual effort to
A. defend one's sister or brother against calumny.
B. fight for one's life against a shark.
C. support the United Nations.
D. defend one's country against an invader.
E. join a volunteer fire fighting association.

82.8
VOCABULARY

To be "qualitatively" different, a feeling must differ in
A. concreteness.
B. abstractness.
C. conception.
D. degree.
E. kind.

Psychology, as the behaviorist views it, is a purely objective, experimental branch of natural science which needs consciousness as little as do the sciences of chemistry and physics. . . . This suggested elimination of states of consciousness as proper objects of investigation in themselves will remove the barrier which exists between psychology and the other sciences. The findings of psychology become the functional correlates of structure and lend themselves to explanation in physico-chemical terms.

───────────── Questions for Passage #83 ─────────────

83.1
SUBJECT MATTER

The passage centers about
A. the nature of consciousness.
B. what the psychologist should investigate.
C. the natural sciences.
D. the behaviorist view of psychology.
E. none of the above.

83.2
GENERALIZATION

According to the author, psychology will become an objective science when
A. it is considered as a branch of natural science.
B. physico-chemical terms are included in explanations of behavior.
C. structure rather than function is made the focus of investigation.
D. consciousness is considered as a proper object of investigation.
E. consciousness is considered outside its province.

83.3
DETAIL

The author feels that psychology should be
A. a natural science.
B. the leading social science.
C. a proper object of investigation.
D. like mathematics.
E. eliminated as a proper object of study.

83.6
APPLICATION

In determining the aptitude of a student for a career as a doctor, the one factor that the author would *not* be apt to rely on would be
A. the student's record of school attendance.
B. the student's score on an intelligence test.
C. the student's score in biology, chemistry, and physics.
D. the student's statement of his career preferences.
E. a knowledge of the occupations of the student's parents, grandparents, etc.

A projectile, if it was not for the force of gravity, would not deviate towards the earth, but would go off from it in a right line, and that with a uniform motion, if the resistance of the air was taken away. It is by its gravity that it is drawn aside continually from its rectilinear course and made to deviate towards the earth, more or less, according to the force of its gravity, and the velocity of its motion. The less its gravity is, or the quantity of its matter, or the greater the velocity with which it is projected, the less will it deviate from a rectilinear course, and the farther it will go. If a leaden ball, projected from the top of a mountain by the force of gunpowder, with a given velocity, and in a direction parallel to the horizon, is carried in a curved line to the distance of two miles before it falls to the ground; the same if the resistance of the air were taken away, with a double or **decuple** velocity, would fly twice or ten times as far. And by increasing the velocity, we may at pleasure increase the distance to which it might be projected, and diminish the curvature of the line which it might describe, till at last it should fall at the distance of 10, 30, or 90 degrees, or even might go quite round the whole earth before it falls; or lastly, so that it might never fall to the earth, but go forwards into the celestial spaces, and proceed in its motion *in infinitum*. And after the same manner that a projectile, by the force of gravity, may be made to revolve in an orbit, and go round the whole earth, the moon also, either by the force of gravity, if it is endued with gravity, or by any other force, that impels it towards the earth, may be continually drawn aside toward the earth, out of the rectilinear way which by its innate force it would pursue, and would be made to revolve in the orbit which it now describes; nor could the moon without some such force be retained in its orbit.

—————— Questions for Passage #84 ——————

**84.1
SUBJECT MATTER**

This passage is mainly concerned with the
A. behavior of projectiles.
B. mathematics of space.
C. control of projectiles.
D. orbit of the moon.
E. the effect of gravity on projectiles.

**84.2
GENERALIZATION**

A major factor which causes bodies to orbit is their tendency to
A. respond to the force of gravity.
B. revolve on their own axis.
C. follow a curved path.
D. lose velocity.
E. deviate from a rectilinear path.

**84.5
CONCLUSION**

One factor that does *not* affect a body's tendency to remain in a rectilinear flight is
A. velocity.
B. air resistance.
C. mass.
D. angle of fall.
E. gravity.

**84.8
VOCABULARY**

The word "decuple" means
A. controlled.
B. tenfold.
C. increased.
D. celestial.
E. fourfold.

I continued this method some few years but gradually left it, retaining only the habit of expressing myself in terms of modest diffidence, never using, when I advanced anything that may possibly by disputed, the words "certainly," "undoubtedly," or any others that give the air of positiveness to an opinion; but rather say, "I should think it so or so for such and such reasons," or "I imagine it to be so," or "It is so if I am not mistaken." This habit I believe has been of great advantage to me when I have had occasion to **inculcate** my opinions and persuade men into measures that I have been from time to time engaged in promoting.   And as the chief ends of conversation are to "inform," or to be "informed," to "please," or to "persuade," I wish well-meaning sensible men would not lessen their power of doing good by a positive assuming manner that seldom fails to disgust, tends to create opposition, and to defeat every one of those purposes for which speech was given to us.   For if you would "inform," a positive, dogmatical manner in advancing your sentiments may provoke contradiction and prevent attention.

_____ Questions for Passage #85 _____

85.4
SIGNIFICANCE

The author of this passage urges us to
A. suggest, rather than insist on, one's opinion.
B. never offend anyone with statements which may provoke contradiction.
C. use a definite approach in informing others of where one stands on an issue.
D. not express sentiments, no matter how strongly felt.
E. hold people's attention by not making definite statements which can be too quickly understood.

85.6
APPLICATION

The approach to the handling of people advocated by the author would be best suited to a
A. military leader.
B. teacher.
C. diplomat.
D. football coach.
E. traffic cop.

85.8
VOCABULARY

In this passage "inculcate" is used to mean
A. retract.
B. mask.
C. regret.
D. change.
E. instill.

Judges are persons appointed to decide all controversies of property, as well as for the trial of criminals, and picked out from the most dexterous lawyers, who are grown old or lazy, and having been biased all their lives against truth and equity, are under such a fatal necessity of favoring fraud, perjury, and oppression, that I have known several of them refuse a large bribe from the side where justice lay, rather than injure the faculty, by doing anything unbecoming their nature or their office.

It is a maxim among lawyers, that whatever hath been done before may legally be done again; and therefore they take special care to record all the decisions formerly made against common justice and the general reason of mankind. These, under the name of precedents they produce as authorities, to justify the most iniquitous opinions; and the judges never fail of directing accordingly. In pleading they studiously avoid entering into the merits of the cause, but are loud, violent, and tedious in dwelling upon all circumstances which are not to the purpose.

It is likewise to be observed, that **this society** hath a peculiar cant and jargon of their own, that no other mortal can understand, and wherein all their laws are written, which they take special care to multiply; whereby they have wholly confounded the very essence of truth and falsehood.

—————— Questions for Passage #86 ——————

86.8 VOCABULARY	By "this society" the author refers to

By "this society" the author refers to
A. the legal profession, including lawyers and judges.
B. judges.
C. lawyers.
D. the people of the time in which this passage was written.
E. those who speak a foreign language.

86.9
COMMUNICATION
TECHNIQUE

The author states that he has "known several . . . (judges) to refuse a large bribe" to
A. be fair to judges.
B. indicate subtly to the reader that he associates with judges.
C. do so as proof of their integrity.
D. demonstrate their contempt for justice.
E. none of the above.

87

No formula for box-office success in a movie is more certain than to have a cocky heroine enter some field which is generally regarded as a masculine **preserve**, achieve some initial superficial successes, and then become so entangled in difficulties that she has to be extricated by the hero, who, smirking forgiveness, offers her his brain for salvation and his lapel for penitence, submission, and tears.

Women in our society are still almost completely dependent upon men for their livelihood, and most of them demonstrate their intelligence by taking care not to seem more intelligent than their escort thinks they ought to be. According to a study of 153 coeds, reported by Mirra Komarovsky in the *American Journal of Sociology*, many college girls deliberately play dumb to please their dates. Forty percent admitted that they lied about their grades, making them out to be lower than they were, gave up arguments when they saw they might win, lost card games, begged for explanations of what they already knew, knowingly misspelled words in their letters and "jigg'd, lisp'd, and ambled" in the manner which so annoyed Prince Hamlet.

─────────────────────────────── Questions for Passage #87 ───────────────────────────────

87.1
SUBJECT MATTER

The subject of this passage is
A. how women adjust to their dependence on men.
B. how college girls fool their dates.
C. the inferiority of women.
D. a formula for box-office success.
E. the intelligence of women in our society.

87.4
SIGNIFICANCE

The author suggests that women's wisest course is to
A. develop their brain power through education.
B. organize to change existing mores.
C. choose men possessed of less intelligence than their own.
D. cultivate the art of pleasing men.
E. develop marketable skills.

87.5
CONCLUSION

The author feels that movies which show women as inferior to men are successful because such inferiority is
A. wishful thinking on the part of men.
B. what women really want.
C. typical of the unreality of movieland.
D. not consciously realized by most women.
E. an accepted social pattern.

87.6
APPLICATION

If he concurred with the thesis of this passge, a legislator attempting to frame a law regulating divorce would probably include provisions to
A. award custody of the children to the women in all cases.
B. make it difficult for incompatible couples to separate.
C. insure payment of alimony to the divorced wife.
D. insure that the court determine the guilty party.
E. do none of the above.

87.8
VOCABULARY

"Preserve" in the context of the passage refers to
A. a condiment.   D. continuation.
B. maintenance.   E. conservation.
C. exclusiveness.

87.9
COMMUNICATION TECHNIQUE

The author mentions that coeds "gave up arguments when they saw they might win, lost card games," etc., to show that women are
A. cowardly.   D. realistic.
B. false.   E. unintelligent.
C. annoying.

88

The institution of government is not a contract, but a law; the **depositaries** of the executive power are not the people's masters, but its officers; it can set them up and pull them down when it likes; for them there is no question of contract, but of obedience; in taking charge of the functions the state imposes on them they are doing no more than fulfilling their duty as citizens; without having the remotest right to argue about the conditions.

———————————— Questions for Passage #88 ————————————

88.1
SUBJECT MATTER

A good title for this selection would be:
A. Law Abiding Citizens.
B. The Servants of the People.
C. The Ways of Government Officials.
D. A Citizen's Rights.
E. Corruption in Government.

88.2
GENERALIZATION

The main thought of this passage is that
A. elected officials should avoid arguments with their constituents.
B. the arrangements between the people and their elected officials resemble a contract in that the people assign their powers to the officials in return for which the officials give their time to directing the peoples' activities.
C. government officials must carry out the desires of the people, rather than seek to have the people carry out their desires.
D. it is the duty of any citizen, when called upon, to act as a public official.
E. government officials have no right to argue about their daily working conditions.

88.8
VOCABULARY

The word "depositaries" means
A. leaders.
B. storehouses.
C. masters.
D. trustees.
E. collectors.

89

In the ethical system of the Greeks, **hubris** — the overweening bumptiousness of individuals or groups in their dealings with other human beings or with the natural order — was regarded as a very grave and, since it invited condign punishment, an extremely dangerous form of delinquency. Monotheism de-sanctified Nature, with the result that, while *hubris* in relation to one's fellow man was still condemned, *hubris* in relation to the non-human environment ceased, under the new dispensation, to be regarded as a sacrilege or a breach of the moral code. And even today, when the consequences of our destructive **bumptiousness** are threatening, through erosion, through deforestation and soil exhaustion, through the progressive pollution and depletion of water resources, to render further human progress ever more difficult, perhaps in a relatively short time impossible — even today the essential wickedness of man's inhumanity to Nature remains unrecognized by the official spokesmen of morality and religion, by practically everyone, indeed, except a few conservationists and ecologists. Acculturated man's "conquest of nature" goes forward at an accelerating pace — a conquest, unfortunately, analogous to that of the most ruthless imperialist exploiters of the colonial period. Man, the species, is now living as a parasite upon an earth which acculturated man is in the process of conquering to the limit — and the limit is total destruction. Intelligent parasites take care not to kill their hosts; unintelligent parasites push their greed to the point of murder and, destroying their own food supply, commit suicide. Boasting all the while of his prowess as a conqueror, but behaving, while he boasts, less intelligently than the flea or even the hookworm, man, the acculturated parasite, is now busily engaged in murdering his host. It is still possible for him to give up his suicidal vampirism and to establish a symbiotic relationship with his natural environment — still possible, but admittedly (with human numbers threatening to double in less than forty years) very difficult. If this very difficult choice is not made, made soon, and made successfully, acculturated man's misdirected cleverness may conquer nature too thoroughly for the survival of his own high culture, perhaps even for the survival of man, the species.

—————————————— Questions for Passage #89 ——————————————

89.2
GENERALIZATION

The author feels that modern man
A. has by his own acts shown a disregard for monotheism.
B. is immoral toward mankind and toward nature.
C. abandoned *hubris* as a way of acting.
D. is a helpless victim of natural destructive forces.
E. feels no moral responsibility toward nature for his acts.

89.3
DETAIL

According to the selection, the belief in monotheism caused a change in man's
A. relationship with nature.   D. view of ecology.
B. relationship with man.   E. attitude toward morality.
C. relationship with society.

89.4
SIGNIFICANCE

The author urges man to establish a symbiotic relationship with his natural environment. This could be achieved through
A. stepping up conservation programs even if man's progress would be stunted.
B. setting up a balanced exchange between man's use of resources and their renewal.
C. developing better ways to make the natural world more productive.
D. solving man's social problems first, and problems of nature second.
E. sharply limiting population expansion.

89.6
APPLICATION

The author would probably be *least* interested in
A. setting up population control.
B. setting aside national wildlife preserves.
C. reforestation measures.
D. a cure for hookworm.
E. a return to the Greek view of man's relation to nature.

89.8 (a)
VOCABULARY

The word "bumptiousness" as used in the selection most nearly means
A. brash self-assertiveness.   D. rusticity.
B. acquisitiveness.   E. chicanery.
C. boorishness.

89.8 (b)
VOCABULARY

"Hubris," as used in the passage, can best be defined as
A. man's attitude toward man.   D. degradation.
B. insolence.   E. delinquency.
C. man's attitude toward nature.

That Man is the product of causes which had no prevision of the end they were achieving, that his origin, his hopes and fears, his loves and his beliefs, are but the outcome of accidental **collocations** of atoms; that no fire, no heroism, no intensity of thought and feeling, can preserve an individual life beyond the grave; that all the labor of the ages, all the devotion, all the inspiration, all the noonday brightness of human genius, are destined to extinction in the vast death of the solar system, and that the whole temple of Man's achievement must inevitably be buried beneath the debris of a universe in ruins — all these things, if not quite beyond dispute, are yet so nearly certain, that no philosophy which rejects them can hope to stand. Only within the scaffolding of these truths, only on the firm foundation of unyielding despair, can the soul's habitation henceforth be safely built.

—————————————————— Questions for Passage #90 ——————————————————

90.5
CONCLUSION

The writer of this passage is most probably
A. a pantheist.
B. an agnostic.
C. a Buddhist.
D. a Christian.
E. an atheist.

90.6
APPLICATION

The passage can be construed as an attack on
A. ideologies which believe in life after death.
B. materialistic philosophies.
C. the scientific interpretation of the universe.
D. philosophies of pessimism and despair.
E. the spiritual values of the 20th Century.

90.8
VOCABULARY

The word "collocations" means
A. collisions.
B. destructions.
C. arrangements.
D. collections.
E. forces.

As long ago as 1670, Montanari noted that the second-magnitude star, Algol, was sometimes fainter than usual. Goodricke, in 1782, discovered that these variations were *periodic* and occurred at regular intervals of $2^d20^h49^m$. For about 2^d11^h the star remains of substantially constant brightness. During the next five hours it loses two-thirds of its light and returns to its original brightness in the five hours following. Goodricke realized that this variation in brightness might be caused by the partial eclipse of the star by a large body revolving round it, but no other **binary stars** were known at that time, and his explanation was almost forgotten until revived by Pickering a century later. Thousands of stars are now definitely known to vary in this fashion.

Like their prototype, Algol, these stars usually remain at a nearly constant magnitude for some time, following which their brightness decreases rapidly to a minimum. The light may remain constant at the minimum for some time or only for a moment, but in either case the increase to normal is as rapid as the decrease. After remaining practically stationary for some time, the brightness falls again, usually much less than before and sometimes almost imperceptibly, then rises again to normal and remains stationary for about the same time as before, after which the whole cycle is repeated with very exact periodicity. The deeper minimum is called the *primary minimum,* the other, the *secondary*.

The difference in brightness between the variable star and a neighboring comparison star of constant brightness is repeatedly measured with a photometer and the time of the observation noted.

This characteristic change in brightness is readily explained on the assumption that the variable star is a binary pair with components usually differing in size and brightness, and that the orbital plane is nearly edgewise to the line of sight from the earth, so that the components eclipse one another during every revolution. When the fainter star begins to pass in front of the brighter, the light from the system begins to decrease.

(NOTE: In the questions which follow (Passages 91-100) the type of question has *not* been shown. Instead, you are asked to take an additional step after finding the answers. *You* are asked to designate the kind of thinking called for by each question.

Questions on each Passage are arranged in random order. After you have selected your answer for each question, *circle* the symbol which designates the type of thinking involved.)

——————————— Questions for Passage #91 ———————————

Answer each question. Then circle the symbol which designates the type of thinking involved.

91-1 **During the period of the primary minimum, the**
A. binary pair is moving away from the earth.
B. plane of the orbit changes.
C. two stars are side by side.
D. fainter star is moving away from the earth.
E. fainter star passes between the earth and the brighter star.
SM G D SIG C A T V CT

91-2 **By "binary star" the author means a**
A. star which is linked with another star by gravity.
B. planet.
C. star with fluctuating brightness.
D. revolving star.
E. second magnitude star.

SM   G   D   SIG   C   A   T   V   CT

91-3 **From the facts given us about the star Algol, we may conclude that Algol's companion star**
A. describes an elliptical orbit around Algol.
B. takes 2^d11^h to complete its orbit around Algol.
C. takes $2^d20^h49^m$ to complete its orbit around Algol.
D. revolves around Algol in a "tumbling" fashion.
E. describes a circular orbit around Algol.

SM   G   D   SIG   C   A   T   V   CT

91-4 **The time for Algol's passage from its maximum brightness through its primary minimum and back again is approximately**
A. 1.5 minutes.
B. 16 minutes.
C. 1.5 hours.
D. 10 hours.
E. 20 hours.

SM   G   D   SIG   C   A   T   V   CT

92

Darwin's cousin, Francis Galton, made the first serious studies in inheritance during the later years of the last century. He collected data of human variations of one sort or another and by a method of mathematical analysis deduced what he claimed were laws of human inheritance. He obtained the height of 204 English parents of graduated statures and their 928 mature children. The average height of females is less than that of males by 8%, so Galton multiplied each female height by 1.08 to bring female height to the same standard as male height. He then added the height of the father to the corrected height of the mother and divided the result by two. This gave him one number for the height of the two parents. He arranged parental heights in classes. The results in inches were as follows.:

	I	II	III	IV	V	VI	VII	VIII	IX
Parental height	64.5	65.5	66.5	67.5	68.5	69.5	70.5	71.5	72.5
Height of children	65.8	66.7	67.2	67.6	68.3	68.9	69.5	69.9	72.2

One notes that the children of the shortest are taller than their parents. This indicates a tendency toward the average height, and is known as "Galton's Law of Filial Regression," which is stated thus: Average parents produce average offspring: tall parents produce tall children, short parents produce short children, but the children are not as tall or as short as their parents, that is, there is a tendency toward the average condition; the children inherit the parental characteristics in a less divers degree. Galton would have this law apply to inheritance of all sorts of characters, mental as well as physical. He made a more definite assertion derived from mathematical consideration of the results, namely, that children show only two-thirds of the parental deviation from the racial average. By his statistical methods he arrived at another general conclusion known as the "Law of Ancestral Inheritance." According to this, he asserted that the two parents contributed one-half of the total inheritance of the child; the four grand-parents, one-fourth; the eight great-grandparents, one-eighth, etc.

—————————————————— Questions for Passage #92 ——————————————————

Answer each question. Then circle the symbol which designates the type of thinking involved.

92-1   **According to Galton's "Law of Filial Regression," the human race will in its future development,**
   A. tend to develop away from present norms of various characteristics.
   B. tend to throw off environmental influences which might change its present norms radically.
   C. tend to develop slowly and gradually away from present norms.
   D. tend to maintain its present norms.
   E. do none of the above.

   SM   G   D   SIG   C   A   T   V   CT

92-2   **According to Galton, your great-grandmother has influenced your heredity to the extent of**
   A. 1/4 of your make-up.   D. 1/128 of your make-up.
   B. 1/16 of your make-up.   E. 1/256 of your make-up.
   C. 1/64 of your make-up.

   SM   G   D   SIG   C   A   T   V   CT

92-3   **Assuming (1) that the average American male dies at 67 years, and the average American female at 69, and (2) that longevity is an inherited characteristic, a man whose parents died at an average of 80 would, according to Galton, most probably die at**
   A. 67.   D. 80.
   B. 69.   E. 85.
   C. 77.

   SM   G   D   SIG   C   A   T   V   CT

In planning a rational future for human communication, we must always ask whether there is not a grain of truth in the conservatism which has obstructed progress. The fact is that some quite reasonable, though insufficient, arguments have been used to oppose the decimal system of measure by mathematicians who for long clung to the old sexagesimal fractions of degrees, minutes, and seconds, and by practical men who were accustomed to measures and weights (like the English monetary system) which go up in multiples of 12. For the purpose of calculation 10 is a bad number, however holy its devotional associations and however venerable its biological antecedents. It has only three exact divisors: 1, 2, 5. The number 12 has 1, 2, 3, 4, 6 as its divisors, and the number 60 has 1, 2, 3, 4, 5, 6, 10, 12, 15, 20, 30. A large number of factors is a great advantage in rapid calculation. So it would be an improvement on our present standards to make a Hegelian compromise of the English and French systems by adding two numbers to the Hindu number script, and making a positional notation based on the twelve-fingered abacus with weights and measures adjusted accordingly. You can make up sums and tables for yourself in the number script with base 12.

$$1 \quad 2 \quad 3 \quad 4 \quad 5 \quad 6 \quad 7 \quad 8 \quad 9 \quad \male \quad \female \quad 10$$
$$(1 \quad 2 \quad 3 \quad 4 \quad 5 \quad 6 \quad 7 \quad 8 \quad 9 \quad 10 \quad 11 \quad 12)$$

―――――――――― Questions for Passage #93 ――――――――――

Answer each question. Then circle the symbol which designates the type of thinking involved.

93-1

The fact that the number 10 has 1, 2, and 5 as its divisors, and the number 12 has 1, 2, 3, 4, and 6 as its divisors, is introduced by the author to

A. bear out why practical men are in favor of the author's recommendation.

B. show why conservative men have obstructed progress.

C. explain the relationship between 10 and 12.

D. strengthen his recommendation of a number system based on 10.

E. strengthen his recommendation of a number system based on 12.

SM   G   D   SIG   C   A   T   V   CT

93-2

The fact that we have ten fingers and ten toes is referred to by the author when he speaks of

A. "reasonable, though insufficient arguments" opposing the number 10.

B. the "devotional associations" of the number 10.

C. "biological antecedents" of the number 10.

D. "the conservatism that has obstructed progress."

E. "a positional notation based on the twelve-fingered abacus."

SM   G   D   SIG   C   A   T   V   CT

93-3

The author's principal contention is that

A. 10 is a bad number to use for calculation because it has only three exact divisors.

B. a number which has the greatest number of factors should be used as the basis of arithmetic calculation.

C. a number system based on 12 rather than 10 would be advantageous.

D. very often conservatism has values which should not be cast aside.

E. the arguments against the decimal system of measures were insufficient because they were advanced by old-time mathematicians and practical men.

SM   G   D   SIG   C   A   T   V   CT

93-4

The Hindu number script apparently

A. includes the signs ♂ and ♀.

B. is a compromise.

C. uses a twelve-fingered abacus.

D. has a base of 10.

E. has a base of 12.

SM   G   D   SIG   C   A   T   V   CT

93-5

For proof in support of his argument for the number base he recommends, the author draws on the field of

A. mathematics.

B. biology.

C. history.

D. political economy.

E. philosophy.

SM   G   D   SIG   C   A   T   V   CT

94

The periodic law was discovered about the year 1870. At the time when it was discovered, the evidence for it was far less complete than it is at present. It has proved itself capable of predicting new elements which have subsequently been found, and altogether the half-century that has passed since its discovery has enormously enhanced its importance. The elements can be arranged in a series by means of what is called their "atomic weight." By chemical methods, we can remove one element from a compound and replace it by an equal number of atoms of another element; we can observe how much this alters the weight of the compound, and thus we can compare the weight of one kind of atom with the weight of another. The lightest atom is that of hydrogen; the heaviest is that of uranium, which weighs over 238 times as much as that of hydrogen. It was found that, taking the weight of the hydrogen atom as one, the weights of a great many other atoms were almost exactly multiples of this unit, so that they were expressed by integers.

The weight of the oxygen atom is a very little less than 16 times that of the hydrogen atom. It has been found convenient to *define* the atomic weight of oxygen at 16, so that the atomic weight of hydrogen becomes slightly more than one (1.008). The advantage of this definition is that it makes the atomic weights of a great many elements whole numbers, within the limits of accuracy that are possible in measurement. The recent work of F. W. Aston on what are called "isotopes" has shown that, in many cases where the atomic weight seems to be not a whole number, we really have a mixture of two different elements, each of which has a whole number for its atomic weight. This is what we should expect if the nuclei of the heavier atoms are composed of the nuclei of hydrogen atoms together with electrons (which are very much lighter than hydrogen nuclei). The fact that so many atomic weights are almost exactly whole numbers cannot be due to chance, and has long been regarded as a reason for supposing that atoms are built up out of smaller units.

Mendeleeff (and at about the same time the German chemist, Lothar Meyer) observed that an element would resemble in its properties, not those that came next to it in the series of atomic weights, but certain other elements which came at periodic intervals in the series. For example, there is a group of elements called "alkalis"; these are the 3rd, 11th, 19th, etc., in the series. These are all very similar in their chemical behavior, and also in certain physical respects, notably their spectrum. Next to these come a group called "alkaline earths"; these are the 4th, 12th, 20th, etc., in the series. The third group are called "earths." There are eight such groups in all. The eighth, which was not known when the law was discovered, is the very interesting group of "inert gases," Helium, Neon, Argon, Krypton, Xenon, and Niton, all discovered since the time of Mendeleeff. These are the 2nd, 10th, 18th, 36th, 54th, and 86th respectively in the series of elements. They all have the property that they will not enter into chemical combinations with any other elements; the Germans, on this account, call them the "noble" gases. The elements from an alkali to the next inert gas form what is called one "period." There are seven periods altogether.

When once the periodic law had been discovered, it was found that a great many properties of elements were periodic. This gave a principle of arrangement of the elements, which in the immense majority of cases placed them in the order of their atomic weights, but in a few cases reversed this order on account of other properties. For example, argon, which is an inert gas, has the atomic weight 39.88, whereas potassium, which is an alkali, has the smaller atomic weight 39.10. Accordingly argon, in spite of its greater atomic weight, has to be placed before potassium, at the end of the third period, while potassium has to be put at the beginning of the fourth. It has been found that, when the order derived from the periodic law differs from that derived from the atomic weight, the order derived from the periodic law is much more important; consequently this order is always adopted.

Answer each question. Then circle the symbol which designates the type of thinking involved.

94-1

Recent research has shown that where the atomic weight does not seem to be a whole number,

A. only parts of atoms have been weighed.

B. the material is a mixture of two elements.

C. the atom is inert.

D. the atom is unstable.

E. the material is an exception to the periodic law.

SM   G   D   SIG   C   A   T   V   CT

94-2

Atomic weight for an element can be determined by

A. definition.

B. multiples of the weight of hydrogen.

C. substitution of elements in a compound.

D. using the atomic weight of oxygen as a base.

E. studying isotopes of an element in combination.

SM   G   D   SIG   C   A   T   V   CT

94-3

The periodic law suggests that two elements are closely related when they

A. occur next to each other in the series of atomic weights.

B. appear as isotopes.

C. are arranged in order of their atomic weights.

D. occur at periodic intervals from each other in the atomic weight series.

E. each are a multiple of the atomic weight of hydrogen.

SM   G   D   SIG   C   A   T   V   CT

94-4

According to the passage, periodic behavior of elements leads scientists to conclude that

A. hydrogen is unique in that its atomic weight is not an integer.

B. man is, for once, the beneficiary of chance factors which have produced order.

C. elements should be arranged by atomic weight rather than by properties.

D. there is a mysterious order in the universe which science cannot explain.

E. all atoms are made up of small units.

SM   G   D   SIG   C   A   T   V   CT

94-5

The atomic weight of copper is 64, that of oxygen is 16. In order to equal the weight of one atom of copper, how many atoms of oxygen are necessary?

A. 1   D. 64

B. 4   E. 128

C. 16

SM   G   D   SIG   C   A   T   V   CT

The Greek's lofty attitude toward scientific research — and the scientists' contempt of utility — was a long time dying. For a millennium after Archimedes, this separation of mechanics from geometry inhibited fundamental technological progress and in some areas repressed it altogether. But there was a still greater obstacle to change until the very end of the middle ages; the organization of society. The social system of fixed class relationships that prevailed through the Middle Ages (and in some areas much longer) itself stultified improvement. Under this system, the laboring masses, in exchange for the bare necessities of life, did all the productive work, while the privileged few — priests, nobles, and kings — concerned themselves only with ownership and maintenance of their own position. In the interest of their prerogatives they did achieve considerable progress in defense, in warmaking, in government, in trade, in the arts of leisure, and in the extraction of labor from their dependents, but they had no familiarity with the processes of production. On the other hand, the laborers, who were familiar with manufacturing techniques, had no incentive to improve or increase production to the advantage of their masters. Thus, with one class possessing the requisite knowledge and experience, but lacking incentive and leisure, and the other class lacking the knowledge and experience, there was no means by which technical progress could be achieved.

The whole ancient world was built upon this relationship — a relationship as sterile as it was inhuman. The availability of slaves nullified the need for more efficient machinery. In many of the commonplace fields of human endeavor, actual stagnation prevailed for thousands of years. Not all the glory that was Greece and the grandeur that was Rome could develop the windmill or contrive so simple an instrument as the wheelbarrow — products of the tenth and thirteenth centuries respectively.

For about twenty-five centuries, two-thirds of the power of the horse was lost because he wasn't shod, and much of the strength of the ox was wasted because his harness wasn't modified to fit his shoulders. For more than five thousand years, sailors were confined to rivers and coasts by a primitive steering mechanism which required remarkably little alteration (in the thirteenth century) to become a rudder.

With any ingenuity at all, the ancient plough could have been put on wheels and the ploughshare shaped to bite and turn the sod instead of merely scratching it — but the ingenuity wasn't forthcoming. And the villager of the Middle Ages, like the men who first had fire, had a smoke hole in the center of the straw and reed thatched roof of his one-room dwelling (which he shared with his animals), while the medieval charcoal burner (like his Stone Age ancestor) made himself a hut of small branches.

_____ Questions for Passage #95 _____

Answer each question. Then circle the symbol which designates the type of thinking involved.

95-1

Lack of technological progress in the ancient and medieval worlds was primarily due to the absence of
A. natural resources.
B. an attitude of respect toward mechanics on the part of philosophers.
C. inventive ability.
D. people's desire for the "better things of life."
E. proper social organization.

SM   G   D   SIG   C   A   T   V   CT

95-2

We may infer that a change in class relationships after the close of the Middle Ages produced greater productivity because
A. freemen had incentive to produce more.
B. masters had greater incentive to work their workers harder.
C. slaves never starved, no matter what they produced.
D. thinkers looked down on utility as a valid subject for thought.
E. productivity could go in only one direction.

SM   G   D   SIG   C   A   T   V   CT

95-3

During the Middle Ages, productivity of labor
A. was a primary concern of society.
B. was hampered by class relationships.
C. began to improve over levels reached by the Greeks.
D. was in a period of technical progress.
E. both increased and decreased.

SM   G   D   SIG   C   A   T   V   CT

95-4

In supporting his contentions about the ancient world, the author relies mainly on illustrations drawn from
A. statements about the deficiencies of the medieval world in the areas of government and war.
B. examples of the separation of mechanics and geometry.
C. technology.
D. case studies of lack of social communication between classes.
E. his concern with the plight of the laboring classes.

SM   G   D   SIG   C   A   T   V   CT

117

To these indirect presumptions that our sensations, following the mutations of our capacity for feeling, are always undergoing an essential change, must be added another presumption, based on what must happen in the brain. Every sensation corresponds to some cerebral action. For an identical sensation to recur it would have to occur the second time *in an unmodified brain.* But as this, strictly speaking, is a physiological impossibility, so is an unmodified feeling an impossibility; for to every brain-modification, however small, we suppose that there must correspond a change of equal amount in the consciousness which the brain subserves.

But if the assumption of "simple sensations" recurring in immutable shape is so easily shown to be baseless, how much more baseless is the assumption of immutability in the larger masses of our thought!

For there it is obvious and palpable that our state of mind is never precisely the same. Every thought we have of a given fact is, strictly speaking, unique, and only bears any resemblance of kind with our other thoughts of the same fact. When the identical fact recurs, we *must* think of it in a fresh manner, see it under a somewhat different angle, apprehend it in different relations from those in which it last appeared. And the thought by which we cognize it is the thought of it-in-those-relations, a thought suffused with the consciousness of all that dim context. Often we are ourselves struck at the strange differences in our successive views of the same thing. We wonder how we ever could have opined as we did last month about a certain matter. We have outgrown the possibility of that state of mind, we know not how. From one year to another we see things in new lights. What was unreal has grown real, and what was exciting is insipid. The friends we used to care the world for are shrunken to shadows; the women once so divine, the stars, the woods, and the waters, how now so dull and common! — the young girls that brought an aura of infinity, at present hardly distinguishable existences; the pictures so empty; and as for the books, what *was* there to find so mysteriously significant in Goethe, or in John Mill so full of weight? Instead of all this, more zestful than ever is the work, the work; and fuller and deeper the import of common duties and of common goods.

Answer each question. Then circle the symbol which designates the type of thinking involved.

96-1   **Our sensations are assumed to change because**
A. the brain changes.
B. no sensation occurs twice in the same way.
C. sensations are complicated.
D. our capacity for feeling remains constant.
E. of none of the above.

SM   G   D   SIG   C   A   T   V   CT

96-2   **We can infer that the writer is**
A. friendless.
B. not a young man.
C. depressed by his findings.
D. dismayed by the changeability of feelings and thoughts.
E. soured on reading great books.

SM   G   D   SIG   C   A   T   V   CT

96-3   **The main idea of this passage is that**
A. we can know sensations only through reasoning, never by direct experience.
B. our mental processes are characterized by change.
C. work is the best goal of man.
D. our past enthusiasms wane with time.
E. each thought is known only in context of our other thoughts.

SM   G   D   SIG   C   A   T   V   CT

96-4   **The author apparently feels that**
A. our values remain constant throughout our lives.
B. our senses are more reliable than our minds.
C. the things we value in our youth are worthless.
D. our reality changes as we change.
E. for any given moment, scientific truth is unobtainable.

SM   G   D   SIG   C   A   T   V   CT

This is the flamelike quality our life has — it is but the concurrence, renewed from moment to moment, of forces parting sooner or later on their ways. . . . Every moment some form grows perfect in hand or face; some tone on the hills or the sea is choicer than the rest; some mood of passion or insight or intellectual excitement is irresistibly real and attractive to us — for that moment only. Not the fruit of experience, but experience itself, is the end. A counted number of pulses only is given to us of a variegated, dramatic life. How may we see in them all that is to be seen in them by the finest senses? How shall we pass most swiftly from point to point, and be present always at the focus where the greatest number of vital forces unite in their purest energy? To burn always with this hard, gem-like flame, to maintain this ecstasy, is success in life. . . . Not to discriminate every moment some passionate attitude in those about us, and in the very brilliancy of their gifts some tragic dividing of forces on their ways, is, on this short day of frost and sun, to sleep before evening. With this sense of the splendor of our experience and of its awful brevity, gathering all we are into one desperate effort to see and touch, we shall hardly have time to make theories about the things we see and touch. . . . We are all "condamnes," as Victor Hugo says: we are all under sentence of death but with a sort of indefinite reprieve: we have an interval, and then our place knows us no more. Some spend this interval in listlessness, some in high passions, the wisest, at least among "the children of this world," in art and song. For our one chance lies in expanding that interval, in getting as many pulsations as possible into the given time. Great passions may give us this quickened sense of life, ecstasy and sorrow of love, the various forms of enthusiastic activity, disinterested or otherwise, which come naturally to many of us. Only be sure it is passion — that it does yield you this fruit of a quickened, multiplied consciousness. Of such wisdom, the poetic passion, the desire of beauty, the love of art for its own sake, has most. For art comes to you proposing frankly to give nothing but the highest quality to your moments as they pass, and simply for those moments' sake.

───────────────── Questions for Passage #97 ─────────────────

Answer each question. Then circle the symbol which designates the type of thinking involved.

97-1   **This author would feel most at home with which of the following cultural goals?**
A. The spiritual preoccupation of the Middle Ages
B. The death-oriented world of the Egyptians
C. The artistic demands of the Impressionist painters of 19th Century France
D. The scientific technological pursuit of the Twentieth Century
E. The Platonic world of static perfection
SM   G   D   SIG   C   A   T   V   CT

97-2   **The author would probably prefer which of the following sentiments?**

A. Beauty is in the eye of the beholder.
B. O, my Luve's like a red red rose
   That's newly sprung in June;
   O, my Luve's like the melodie
   That's sweetly play'd in tune.
C. Heard melodies are sweet, but those unheard
   Are sweeter; therefore, ye soft pipes, play on;
   Not to the sensual ear, but more endear'd
   Pipe to the spirit ditties of no tone . . .
D. Keep your shop and your shop will keep you.
E. Man does not live by bread alone.
   SM   G   D   SIG   C   A   T   V   CT

97-3   **In his attitude toward life, the author can best be described as**

A. a stoic.   D. an erotic.
B. a sensualist.   E. an epicure.
C. an esthete.
   SM   G   D   SIG   C   A   T   V   CT

97-4   **The author urges the reader to**

A. achieve as many experiences of beauty as possible.
B. gain as much experience as possible.
C. plan for the future.
D. create art.
E. live dangerously.
   SM   G   D   SIG   C   A   T   V   CT

98

It is notorious that facts are compatible with opposite emotional comments, since the same fact will inspire entirely different feelings in different persons, and at different times in the same person; and there is no rationally deducible connection between any outer fact and the sentiments it may happen to provoke. These have their source in another sphere of existence altogether, in the animal and spiritual region of the subject's being. Conceive yourself, if possible, suddenly stripped of all the emotion with which your world now inspires you, and try to imagine it *as it exists*, purely by itself, without your favorable or unfavorable, hopeful or apprehensive comment. It will be almost impossible for you to realize such a condition of negativity and deadness. No one portion of the universe would then have importance beyond another; and the whole collection of its things and series of its events would be without significance, character, expression, or perspective. Whatever of value, interest, or meaning our respective worlds may appear endowed with are thus pure gifts of the spectator's mind. The passion of love is the most familiar and extreme example of this fact. If it comes, it comes; if it does not come, no process of reasoning can force it. Yet it transforms the value of the creature loved as utterly as the sunrise transforms Mont Blanc from a corpse-like gray to a rosy enchantment; and it

Go on to next page. ➤

sets the whole world to a new tune for the lover and gives a new issue to his life. So with fear, with indignation, jealousy, ambition, worship. If they are there, life changes. And whether they shall be there or not depends almost always upon non-logical, often on organic conditions. And as the excited interest which these passions put into the world is our gift to the world, just so are the passions themselves *gifts*; — gifts to us, from sources sometimes low and sometimes high; but almost always non-logical and beyond our control. How can the **moribund** old man reason back to himself the romance, the mystery, the imminence of great things with which our old earth tingled for him in the days when he was young and well? Gifts, either of the flesh or of the spirit; and the spirit bloweth where it listeth; and the world's materials lend their surface passively to all the gifts alike, as the stage-setting receives indifferently whatever alternating colored lights may be shed upon it from the optical apparatus in the gallery.

Meanwhile the practically real world for each one of us, the effective world of the individual, is the compound world, the physical facts and emotional values in indistinguishable combination. Withdraw or pervert either factor of this complex resultant, and the kind of experience we call pathological ensues.

—————————————— Questions for Passage #98 ——————————————

Answer each question. Then circle the symbol which designates the type of thinking involved.

98-1   **We can conclude from the passage that a man who is about to be executed will feel**

A. depressed.   D. confused.
B. elated.   E. emotions we cannot predict.
C. apathetic.

SM   G   D   SIG   C   A   T   V   CT

98-2   **Our feelings about external reality have their genesis in**

A. gifts we receive from others.   D. our health.
B. events that affect us personally.   E. our subjective being.
C. our immediate environment.

SM   G   D   SIG   C   A   T   V   CT

98-3   **A "moribund" old man is one who is**

A. dying.   D. apathetic.
B. prosaic.   E. unloved.
C. experienced.

SM   G   D   SIG   C   A   T   V   CT

98-4   **The passion of love is cited by the author to show how**

A. unable we are to control our emotions.
B. our world can be transformed by our feelings.
C. unreal our practical world is.
D. easy it is to understand passions when we have experienced love.
E. familiar passions are to us.

SM   G   D   SIG   C   A   T   V   CT

The phenomena of selective attention and of deliberative will are of course patent examples of this choosing activity. But few of us are aware how incessantly it is at work in operations not ordinarily called by these names. Accentuation and Emphasis are present in every perception we have. We find it quite impossible to disperse our attention impartially over a number of impressions. A monotonous succession of sonorous strokes is broken up into rhythms, now of one sort, now of another, by the different accent which we place on different strokes. The simplest of these rhythms is the double one, tick-tock, tick-tock, tick-tock. Dots dispersed on a surface are perceived in rows and groups. Lines separate into diverse figures. The **ubiquity** of the distinctions, *this* and *that*, *here* and *there*, *now* and *then*, in our minds is the result of our laying the same selective emphasis on parts of place and time.

But we do far more than emphasize things, and unite some, and keep others apart. We actually *ignore* most of the things before us. Let me briefly show how this goes on.

To begin at the bottom, what are our very senses themselves, but organs of selection? Out of the infinite chaos of movement, of which physics teaches us that the outer world consists, each sense-organ picks but those which fall within certain limits of velocity. To these it responds, but ignores the rest as completely as if they did not exist. Out of what is in itself an undistinguishable, swarming *continuum*, devoid of distinction or emphasis, our senses make for us, by attending to this motion and ignoring that, a world full of contrasts, of sharp accents, of abrupt changes, of picturesque light and shade.

If the sensations we receive from a given organ have their causes thus picked out for us by the conformation of the organ's termination, Attention, on the other hand, out of all the sensations yielded, picks out certain ones as worthy of notice, and suppresses all the rest. We notice only those sensations which are signs to us of *things* which happen practically or aesthetically to interest us, to which we therefore give substantive names, and which we exalt to this exclusive status of independence and dignity. But in itself, apart from my interest, a particular dust-wreath on a windy day is just as much of an individual *thing*, and just as much or as little deserves an individual name, as my own body does.

Go on to next page. ➤

And then, among the sensations we get from each separate thing, what happens? The minds selects again. It chooses certain of the sensations to represent the things most *truly*, and considers the rest as its appearances, modified by the conditions of the moment. Thus my table-top is named *square*, after but one of an infinite number of retinal sensations which it yields, the rest of them being sensations of two acute and two obtuse angles; but I call the latter *perspective* views, and the four right angles the *true* form of the table, and erect the attribute squareness into the table's essence, for aesthetic reasons of my own. In like manner, the real form of the circle is deemed to be the sensation it gives when the line of vision is perpendicular to its center — all its other sensations are *signs* of this sensation. The real sound of the cannon is the sensation it makes when the ear is close by. The real color of the brick is the sensation it gives when the eye looks squarely at it from a near point, out of the sunshine and yet not in the gloom; under other circumstances it gives us other color-sensations which are but signs of this — we then see it looks pinker or bluer than it really is. The reader knows no object which he does not represent to himself by preference as in some typical attitude, of some normal size, at some characteristic distance, or some standard tint, etc., etc. But all these essential characteristics, which together form for us the genuine objectivity of the thing and are contrasted with what we call the subjective sensations it may yield us at a given moment, are mere sensations like the latter. The mind chooses to suit itself, and decides what particular sensation shall be held more real and valid than all the rest.

Next, in a world of objects thus individualized by our mind's selective industry, what is called our "experience" is almost entirely determined by our habits of attention. A thing may be present to a man a hundred times, but if he persistently fails to notice it, it cannot be said to enter into his experience. We are all seeing flies, moths, and beetles by the thousand, but to whom, save an entomologist, do they say anything distinct? On the other hand, a thing met only once in a lifetime may leave an indelible experience in the memory. Let four men make a tour in Europe. One will bring home only picturesque impressions — costumes and colors, parks and views and works of architecture, pictures and statues. To another all this will be non-existent; and distances and prices, populations and drainage-arrangements, door- and window-fastenings, and other useful statistics will take their place. A third will give a rich account of the theaters, restaurants, and public halls, and naught besides; whilst the fourth will perhaps have been so wrapped in his own subjective broodings as to be able to tell little more than a few names of places through which he passed. Each has selected, out of the same mass of presented objects, those which suited his private interest and has made his experience thereby.

Answer each question. Then circle the symbol which designates the type of thinking involved.

99-1   **Out of the swarming continuum of the outer world, our sense organs pick up stimuli which are**

A. agreeable.   D. picturesque.

B. disagreeable.   E. speeded up.

C. within certain limits of velocity.

                  SM   G   D   SIG   C   A   T   V   CT

99-2   **The best title for this selection would be:**

A. Shaping Reality.

B. Paying Attention Is Important.

C. The Continuum of Stimuli.

D. Our Senses, Windows to the World.

E. Mind Over Matter.

                  SM   G   D   SIG   C   A   T   V   CT

99-3   **Mental factors operative in shaping human experience are the mind's decisions, which we can call "will" and "attention." Another basic factor in shaping experience is held to be**

A. the memory.

B. experiences we consistently ignore.

C. subjective sensations.

D. our propensity to anthropomorphize.

E. the nature of the sense organs.

                  SM   G   D   SIG   C   A   T   V   CT

99-4   **We may conclude from this passage that words in the unabridged dictionary represent**

A. objects that have a practical use for man.

B. objects that interest man.

C. objects which exist apart from whether or not man gives them recognition.

D. almost all the objects that exist in the real world.

E. objects of physical substance.

                  SM   G   D   SIG   C   A   T   V   CT

99-5   **The author uses the example of the table to show that**

A. most table tops are square.

B. the mind selects only one of many stimuli to represent a table.

C. the mind does not always see a table in perspective.

D. the table has an independent objective existence.

E. external objects are impermanent.

                  SM   G   D   SIG   C   A   T   V   CT

99-6   **The "ubiquity" of the distinctions mentioned refers to their being**

A. imaginative.   D. subjective.

B. unreal.   E. obvious.

C. everywhere.

                  SM   G   D   SIG   C   A   T   V   CT

The table before which we sit may be, as the scientist maintains, composed of dancing atoms, but it does not reveal itself to us as anything of the kind, and it is not with dancing atoms but a solid and motionless object that we live. So remote is this "real" table — and most of the other "realities" with which science deals — that it cannot be discussed in terms which have any human value, and though it may receive our purely intellectual credence it cannot be woven into the pattern of life as it is led, in contradistinction to life as we attempt to think about it. Vibrations in the ether are so totally unlike, let us say, the color purple that the gulf between them cannot be bridged, and they are, to all intents and purposes, not one but two separate things of which the second and less "real" must be the most significant for us. And just as the sensation which has led us to attribute an **objective reality** to a non-existent thing which we call "purple" is more important for human life than the conception of vibrations of a certain frequency, so too the belief in God, however ill founded, has been more important in the life of man than the germ theory of decay, however true the latter may be.

We may, if we like, speak of consequence, as certain mystics love to do, of the different levels or orders of truth. We may adopt what is essentially a Platonistic trick of thought and insist upon postulating the existence of external realities which correspond to the needs and modes of human feeling and which, so we may insist, have their being in some part of the universe unreachable by science. But to do so is to make an unwarrantable assumption and to be guilty of the metaphysical fallacy of failing to distinguish between a truth of feeling and that other sort of truth which is described as a "truth of correspondence," and it is better perhaps, at least for those of us who have grown up in an age of scientific thought, to steer clear of such confusions and to rest content with the admission that, though the universe with which science deals is the real universe, yet we do not and cannot have any but fleeting and imperfect contacts with it; that the most important part of our lives — our sensations, emotions, desires, and aspirations — takes place in a universe of illusions which science can attenuate or destroy, but which it is powerless to enrich.

Answer each question. Then circle the symbol which designates the type of thinking involved.

100-1   **The author suggests that in order to bridge the puzzling schism between scientific truth and the world of illusion, the reader should**
A. try to rid himself of his world of illusion.
B. accept his world as being one of illusion.
C. apply the scientific method.
D. learn to acknowledge both.
E. establish a truth of correspondence.
SM   G   D   SIG   C   A   T   V   CT

100-2   **Judging from the ideas and tone of the selection, one may reasonably guess that the author is**
A. a humanist.
B. a pantheist.
C. a nuclear physicist.
D. a doctor of medicine.
E. a writer of popular articles on science.
SM   G   D   SIG   C   A   T   V   CT

100-3   **According to this passage, a scientist would conceive of a "table" as being**
A. a solid motionless object.
B. certain characteristic vibrations in "ether."
C. a form fixed in space and time.
D. a mass of atoms in motion.
E. a platform to put an object on.
SM   G   D   SIG   C   A   T   V   CT

100-4   **The topic of this selection is**
A. the distortion of reality by science.
B. the confusion caused by emotions.
C. Platonic and contemporary views of truth.
D. a scientific approach to living.
E. the place of scientific truth in our lives.
SM   G   D   SIG   C   A   T   V   CT

100-5   **By "objective reality" the author means**
A. scientific reality.
B. a symbolic existence.
C. the viewer's experience.
D. reality colored by emotion.
E. a phenomenon we can directly experience.
SM   G   D   SIG   C   A   T   V   CT